W9-BTL-202

THE LOVE THAT NEVER ENDS

A Key to the Catechism of the Catholic Church

J. Augustine DiNoia, O.P.

Gabriel O'Donnell, O.P.

Romanus Cessario, O.P.

Peter John Cameron, O.P.

Our Sunday Visitor Publishing Division
Our Sunday Visitor, Inc.
Huntington, Indiana 46750

International Standard Book Number: 0-87973-852-9
Library of Congress Catalog Card Number: 96-68289

Cover design by Monica Watts
Printed in the United States of America

852

Abbreviations

CCEO	*Corpus Canonum Ecclesiarum Orientalium* (Canons of the Eastern Churches)
CIC	*Codex Iuris Canonici* (Code of Canon Law)
CT	*Catechesi tradendae* (Apostolic Exhortation on Catechesis)
DS	Denzinger-Schönmetzer, *Enchiridion Symbolorum, definitionum et declarationum de rebus fidei et morum* (Handbook of dogmas and creeds)
GS	*Gaudium et spes* (Constitution on the Church in the Modern World)
LG	*Lumen gentium* (Dogmatic Constitution on the Church)
PG	*Patrologia Graeca*, J. P. Migne, ed. (Writings of the Greek [Eastern] Fathers)
PL	*Patrologia Latina*, J. P. Migne, ed. (Writings of the Latin [Western] Fathers)
RSV	*Revised Standard Version* of the Bible
SC	*Sacrosanctum concilium* (Constitution on the Sacred Liturgy)
STh	*Summa theologiae* (A summary of theology)
UR	*Unitatis redintegratio* (Decree on Ecumenism)
VS	*Veritatis splendor* (The Splendor of Truth)

Table of Contents

Foreword

I am very pleased to present this small commentary on the *Catechism of the Catholic Church*, which I am confident will help many parents, religious educators, and clergy open up the riches of the new Catechism to those entrusted to their care.

The Catechism stands on four foundational pillars: the Creed, the Sacraments, the Commandments, and the Our Father. The choice of these four pillars is not arbitrary, but comes from a reflection on the Church's baptismal practice. In order to receive Baptism, what must a catechumen know? Following centuries of the Church's catechetical experience, the *Rite of Christian Initiation for Adults* provides the answer: In order to receive Baptism and the other sacraments of the Christian life, one must first know the basics of Christian belief (Creed), the elements of both Christian conduct (the Commandments) and worship (the sacraments of the New Law), and the rudiments of Christian prayer (the Our Father).

Sometimes catechetical instruction places the commandments before the sacraments. But the new Catechism follows the example of the 1566 Roman Catechism that was issued after the Council of Trent and puts the sacraments first. This ordering implies an important truth for Christian life and catechesis: All efforts to lead a Christian moral life inevitably fail without the grace of the Holy Spirit given through the sacraments. Jesus himself reminds us that "apart from me you can do nothing" (cf. Jn 15:5). Because Christ offers us a love that never ends, our efforts to lead a good life never go unsupported.

Drawing up a catechism for the universal Church was a bold undertaking. In a world of cultural division, political differences, and religious pluralism, can the Church still hope to produce a single, worldwide, Church-wide text for catechesis? It was my privilege to address this question at the 1985 Synod of Bishops: "We have to teach faith in a world that daily becomes more and more a global village." Let me continue by citing the official Latin of the synod hall: "*Juvenes Bostoniensis, Leningradiensis, et Sancti Jacobi in Chili induti sunt 'Blue Jeans' et audiunt et saltant eandem musicam.*" While Latinists may wince, many bishops recognized the truth that since young people in Boston, St. Petersburg, and Santiago, Chile, wear the same blue jeans and dance to the same music, they should also learn from the same catechism.

The Christian faith teaches a single Truth. The unity of faith is neither a vague idea nor an abstract ideal; it is a living reality. Because the truth is preached all over the world, the unity of the faith requires common expressions, no matter what other differences exist among peoples. Indeed, the universal call to holiness that Christian faith imparts represents one of the wonders of God's plan for our salvation. It is because we are all bound for the same glory, that we all need to follow the same Truth.

Faith is not only one in space, it is one also in time. So the Catechism pays special attention to tradition, that is, the identity of the faith that Christ passed on to his Apostles and from them to generation after generation. The Christian message is reliable because it truthfully represents the faith of the Apostles, handed on in the Church — through writing and proclamation — as the most precious gift of the Lord. St. Irenaeus reminds us that this transmission is never like a "mechanical handing on of bricks," but forms a living tradition always renewed by the Holy Spirit.

The purpose of any catechism, and especially of the new Catechism, remains the faithful transmission of the apostolic faith. Of course, there exists a development of Christian doctrine. But the very nature of a catechism requires that it stress the continuity of faith that undergirds the course of its development. I would like to point out another example of continuity: this "Key" to the Catechism comes from the pen of four Dominican Fathers, whose Order, especially in the person of Pope St. Pius V, was actively involved in the preparation of the 1566 Roman Catechism.

St. Thomas Aquinas, who insists on the importance of the expressions of faith, also teaches that the unity of faith moves beyond simple agreement about words. Christ Jesus himself is the living cornerstone, and it is our life in him that ultimately guarantees the only true universality. The transmission of the one faith remains a matter of life and salvation. Not by accident does the *Catechism* of the Second Vatican Council open with the same Scripture used by the *Catechism* of the Council of Trent: "And eternal life is this: to know you, the only true God, and Jesus Christ whom you have sent" (Jn 17:3). Accordingly, the 1994 Catechism aims to set forth the "fullness of Christ" within the context of Trinitarian communion. There can be no doubt that the conciliar Christocentrism of the *Catechism of the Catholic Church* inspires the present commentary. My prayer is that this "Key" will help Christian believers everywhere to embrace the Love that never ends, so that they will come to the glorious inheritance that is promised to those who know the Father, the Son, and the Holy Spirit.

Bernard Cardinal Law
30 April 1996
Feast of Pope St. Pius V

Introduction

The Love That Never Ends

All of us have had the experience of wanting things and working very hard to get them. A son wants the latest video game or a daughter wants the newest style of running shoes. Electronics companies design compact radios and televisions; computer companies release fabulous software, and we all want to have them.

In itself, this observation need not be a cause for lament — unless, of course, we become consumed with a materialistic hankering and ignore the needs of others and our own need for greater goods than these. The Catholic tradition teaches us that, in itself, there is nothing wrong with acquiring and enjoying the good things of this world. Indeed, if we cannot enjoy these good things, how can we be sure that we will enjoy their Maker?

The point is this: To observe that we all want things and work hard to possess them can lead us to an important insight about ourselves — provided that we go on to observe what typically happens next. Often, after wanting, seeking, and acquiring those new shoes and that new software, we get tired of them. Our homes have closets and drawers full of toys that our children wanted badly and soon tired of, clothes that we never wear, radios with dead batteries, and software that we lost interest in. For no amount of wanting, pursuing, and possessing can make us happy once and for all. Certainly, we know that no object can make us happy in that way. Only the love we share with our husbands and wives, with our sons and daughters, mothers and fathers, brothers and sisters can even begin to approach the quality of an ultimately satisfying good. But we also have to admit to ourselves that even these great and consuming loves do not finally fulfill the longing in our hearts.

No one has said more clearly than St. Augustine what all this means in the light of the Gospel: "Our hearts are restless until they rest in You." No created good can ever satisfy hearts that were made to want, seek, and enjoy the uncreated Good. The God who made us to enjoy the good things of this world, and to seek our happiness in the love of other persons, intends for us to enjoy a beatitude large enough to satisfy the infinite longing of the human heart and mind for goodness and truth. That goodness and truth are nothing less than the Goodness and Truth who are the three Persons of the Blessed Trinity, Father, Son, and Holy Spirit. It is God's intention to share nothing less than this personal communion with us.

The *Catechism of the Catholic Church* in all its parts insists that we must never settle for less than this. Jesus Christ makes possible for us a participation in the communion of divine life and love that is as great as any that could be shared with created persons by the uncreated Persons of the Trinity. No more intimate engagement with the three-personed God is possible for creaturely persons.

The presentation of the Christian faith in the eight hundred pages of the Catechism is far from being a dry and abstract rehearsal of doctrines. Rather, it establishes the point and focus of human life within the all-embracing plan of divine providence: nothing less than ultimate communion. Quoting the Catechism of the Council of Trent, the new Catechism takes as its "pastoral principle" this remarkable statement: "The whole concern of doctrine and its teaching must be directed to the love that never ends. Whether something is proposed for belief, for hope or for action, the love of our Lord must always be made accessible, so that anyone can see that all the works of perfect Christian virtue spring from love and have no other objective than to arrive at love" (25; Roman Catechism, Preface, 10; cf. I Cor 13:8).

The object of the chapters that follow is simply to unlock the inner meaning of the many truths proposed in the Catechism by using this single truth as the key: to share in the unending love of the triune God is the destiny of every human person in Christ. With the Catechism itself, this book seeks to move the reader to understand and embrace, in the words of our Holy Father, this "stunning truth" about our destiny in Christ.

There is no attempt here to summarize the contents of the Catechism, or to explain every detail of the doctrines it presents. There is no substitute for reading and pondering the Catechism itself.

Rather, the object of this book is to display the organic unity that underlies the Catechism's presentation of the Christian faith. Each of the four pillars of the Catechism, despite their distinctive contents, is about a single mystery. The mystery that transforms our thinking through the *creed* nourishes our personal and communal lives through the *liturgy and sacraments*, reshapes our character and conduct through the *commandments*, and reorients our entire lives through *prayer*. It is the one mystery of the love that never ends, the three-personed Love that calls us to new life. As the Catechism itself affirms: "There is an organic connection between our spiritual life and the dogmas. Dogmas are lights along the path of faith; they illuminate it and make it secure. Conversely, if our life is upright, our intellect and heart will be open to welcome the light shed by the dogmas of faith" (89; cf. Jn 8:31-32).

The following chapters prompt the reader to look beneath the divisions of the Catechism's presentation of the faith in order to grasp its underlying organic unity and to enjoy the integral vision of the faith to which it so masterfully affords us access — nothing less than the mystery of the triune God.

If we are to understand and use the Catechism properly, we must see the person of Christ at its heart. The Catechism aims to put us in touch with Jesus Christ: "only he can lead us to the love of the Father in the Spirit and make us share in the life of the Holy Trinity" (426; CT 5).

No created good — whether material or personal — can satisfy hearts that were made to enjoy the love that never ends. The Catechism summons us never to settle for less.

Chapter 1

The Catechism: The Echo of Christ's Voice

This is an historic moment in the life of the Church. Not since the Roman Catechism of the Council of Trent was promulgated by Pope St. Pius V in the sixteenth century has a major catechism been composed for the universal Church. In the aftermath of the Second Vatican Council, the circumstances are different, surely, and the universal Church is bigger and far more culturally diverse than it was at the time of the Council of Trent. But, along with the bishops of the Church, Pope John Paul II sees these final years before the dawn of the coming millennium as a time to reaffirm our faith, to renew our Catholic life, and to commit ourselves to the new evangelization. In presenting the Catechism to the Church, our Holy Father wrote that "it will make a very important contribution to that work of renewing the whole life of the Church, as desired and begun by the Second Vatican Council."

A Catechism for the Universal Church

It is no secret that some people doubted whether it would be possible these days to compose a catechism for the universal Church. Given the tremendous diversity of language and culture that marks the Catholic Church today, it seemed to some people that an attempt to express the faith in one universally applicable volume would be counterproductive, if not actually impossible to achieve.

In fact, however, these are precisely the kinds of circumstances that demand a universal catechism. The Catechism is a natural response on the Church's part to the contemporary challenge to affirm a universally valid faith in the midst of cultural and religious diversity. It is one of the deepest of Catholic convictions that the faith is universally expressible and communicable because God's purposes in creation and redemption are universal — encompassing, yet transcending, history and culture. The Catechism proclaims and articulates a faith that is in continuity with the apostles and that embraces all of humankind in a single communion of hope and love.

There have been many catechisms in the history of the Church, to be sure. The need for accessible and readable compendia of the faith has been recognized almost from the beginning. The earliest catechism dates from the second century. St. Augustine wrote a catechism in the fifth century, and his example was followed by other saints and theologians, like St. Thomas Aquinas in the thirteenth and St. Robert Bellarmine in the sixteenth. Often, catechisms — like our own well-known Baltimore Catechism — were composed for local churches, in order to respond to particular needs and circumstances. As major catechisms, the *Catechism of the Catholic Church*, and the Roman Catechism before it, are unique in the role they play in expressing the faith of the universal Church, the Church that embraces all times and cultures. Thus, while the Catechism does not replace or supplant local catechisms, it will serve as a standard or reference text for the development of such catechisms, just as the Roman Catechism did in the past.

Catechesis and the Catechism

Before there were catechisms, there was "catechesis." The meaning of this term throws light on the nature of Christian catechesis and its expression in catechisms.

The term derives from the usage of the ancient Greek theater where it meant "to make resound like an echo." It was first employed in a Christian context in the Acts of the Apostles and in the Letters of St. Paul to refer to the responsibility to form new disciples in the way of Christ. The usage is significant. The one who proclaims and teaches the faith is echoing what he or she has learned from Christ. At the same time, this catechesis is intended to produce an echo in the heart and mind of the listener. It is the echo of the voice of Christ himself, whose word and grace transform the knowledge and life of the one who listens to him.

The etymology of the term "catechesis" teaches us something very important about the kind of knowledge the Catechism expresses and imparts.

A catechism is not just a compendium of useful knowledge, like a biology textbook or a computer manual. Certainly, it is like such books in trying to present the full range of Christian belief and practice in an accessible, accurate, and comprehensive manner. But, more than this, in the Catechism, the voice of Christ calls out to the heart and mind of believers, or of the seekers, summoning them to a new life of communion with the Father, Son, and Holy Spirit, and with one another in them. The knowledge that is imparted by the Catechism is thus a truly personal knowledge. In line with all authentic Christian catechesis, the Catechism is meant to help us to know more about the Christ whom we already know as the risen Lord who abides with us.

For this reason, too, the Catechism is not a substitute for the Scriptures, but opens our minds to their full meaning.

While it is true, then, that the Church and her teachers transmit this knowledge in kerygma (proclamation) and catechesis (instruction), they do so only as the echo of Christ himself and only in order to produce an echo of his voice in our hearts and minds. He is the first teacher, and all the rest are learners and disciples. If any of us teach in his name — whether as catechists, or parents, or theologians, or bishops — it is still Christ whom we commend, and not ourselves.

Life on High in Christ Jesus

Just looking at the way the Catechism is organized makes these fundamental truths vividly clear. The creed, or "profession of faith," comes first. Why? We would have nothing to say as Christians if the Father had not spoken through the Son and in the Holy Spirit, calling us into communion with them. The contents of the articles of the Apostles' Creed amount in the end to a simple, but glorious affirmation: the uncreated Persons of the blessed Trinity call out in love to created persons to summon us to ultimate communion and to enable us to enjoy this communion.

What comes next in the Catechism is not the commandments, as one might expect. Rather, part two of the Catechism presents the sacraments. The natural human response to hearing the affirmation of the triune God's invitation to communion would be to want to do something about it, to wonder how to respond in a concrete way to this invitation. The structure of the Catechism in effect tells us that, by ourselves, we cannot respond to this invitation. God himself makes it possible for us to respond through the manifold grace of the sacraments through which Christ works to conform us to himself so that the Father "might see and love in us what [he sees and loves] in Christ."

Only in the light of the transforming and enabling grace of Christ can we speak about the Ten Commandments and the Beatitudes which form the substance of part three of the Catechism. The high moral ideals of the Christian life can be pursued and attained only through the grace of Christ who empowers us to live human life at a new, or supernatural, level and who forgives our sins and helps us to overcome their bad effects on our character and actions.

Then, in part four of the Catechism, we see an anticipation of the goal of Christian life — easy communication and communion with the Father, through Christ and in the Spirit. The Our Father captures the moment of communion between the triune God and the believer. The experience of prayer both expresses the communion we already share through the indwelling Holy Spirit and provides us with a foretaste of its consummation in "life on high in Christ Jesus" (cf. Phil 3:14).

Knowledge and Experience

In effect, then, the presentation of our Catholic faith in the Catechism is far from being a dry and abstract rehearsal of doctrines. Rather, it seeks to establish the very point and focus of human life within the all-embracing plan of divine providence: nothing less than ultimate communion. The Catechism insists that, in our understanding and teaching of the Catholic faith, we never settle for less than this.

An underlying premise of the Catechism is that knowledge of this great destiny, as it is detailed in the doctrines of the Catholic faith, is fundamental to authentic Christian experience.

The implication here is that a certain range of experiences is possible only when one possesses the requisite knowledge. We are more familiar with the idea that certain things can be learned only by experience. This is a great truth. There are things that can only be learned by experience. Furthermore, it is also the case that experience is fundamental to learning in religion, as in other areas of life. You cannot learn how to use a computer just by reading a book about it. You must start tapping at the keys, trying to produce a text or even just a simple sentence.

But consider a truth that is somewhat less familiar. There are a lot of situations where knowledge makes the enjoyment of certain experiences possible, and the lack of requisite knowledge precludes this enjoyment. Consider a mundane example. If you know nothing about football, can you enjoy watching a game on television? You might find it entertaining to watch people crashing into each other. But you can neither understand nor play football without at least a rudimentary grasp of its rules. The rules and strategies of the game are anything but simple. The running commentary that accompanies televised football games makes it clear just how elaborate these rules are, and reveal that seemingly haphazard movements on the field are in fact meticulously calculated and rehearsed.

This example, and many others that could be given, suggest that knowledge is a condition for the enjoyment of certain kinds of experience. This point is of the greatest importance for understanding the role of knowledge in the religious realm.

While it is true that Christianity is concerned with a lot more than knowledge, it is nonetheless also true that knowledge, whether acquired or infused, affords the enjoyment of experiences otherwise not only impossible but also unimaginable. A conviction about this is crucial to the Christian impulse to catechesis, proclamation, and formation. In effect, the Catechism supplies the kind of knowledge that helps to make the experience of ultimate communion possible.

In his apostolic letter on preparation for the jubilee year of 2000 (*Tertio millennio adveniente*), Pope John Paul II writes that "in Jesus Christ God not only speaks to man but also seeks him out" (7). The power and effectiveness of the Catechism can be understood only in the light of the deep conviction that, through it, the voice of Christ can be heard speaking of God and seeking out every human person. That there can be a universally expressible and communicable faith, a faith that can be proclaimed in every time and in all cultures, rests finally on the truth that the voice of Christ has the power to touch every human heart and to transform every human mind. Perhaps it is not so difficult to understand, in the light of this truth, the huge popularity that the Catechism has enjoyed worldwide since its publication. Surely, it is with this truth that any authentic interpretation and understanding of the Catechism must begin.

Chapter 2

The Legacy of Vatican Council II

Can the *Catechism of the Catholic Church* be called the Catechism of Vatican II? In a real sense, it deserves to be.

When the only previous major catechism was presented to the whole Catholic Church, its official title — *Catechismus ex Decreto Concilii Tridentini ad Parochos* — indicated that it was prepared and published under the explicit mandate of the Council of Trent.

The Catechism and Vatican II

Four hundred years later, some of the Fathers at the Second Vatican Council suggested that a new major catechism might be a good idea. But, in the end, the consensus was that it would be wiser to give the teachings of the council some time to be pondered and absorbed by the Church before they could be codified in the form of a major catechism.

In observance of the twentieth anniversary of the close of the Second Vatican Council in 1985, the general assembly of the Synod of Bishops gathered to celebrate, in the words of Pope John Paul II, "the graces and spiritual fruits of Vatican II, to study its teaching in greater depth in order that all the Christian faithful might better adhere to it and promote knowledge and application of it." The time now seemed ripe for a catechism that would capture this teaching and spirit.

So it was that the Synod Fathers announced: "Very many have expressed the desire that a catechism or compendium of all catholic doctrine regarding both faith and morals be composed, . . . a point of reference for the catechisms and compendiums that are prepared in various regions. The presentation of doctrine must be biblical and liturgical. It must be sound doctrine suited to the present life of Christians." When, after nearly ten years of work, the new Catechism could be presented to the Church, our Holy Father expressed the confidence of all the bishops that it would "make a very important contribution to that work of renewing the whole life of the Church, as desired and begun by the Second Vatican Council."

Thus, even though it was not explicitly mandated by the Council, the Catechism deserves to be called, at least unofficially, the "Catechism of Vatican II."

For one thing, the Catechism incorporates extensive quotations from all of the documents of the Second Vatican Council. It thus provides a real synthesis of the teaching of the council in a way that is topical and accessible.

In addition, several features of the composition and contents of the Catechism reflect the conciliar legacy.

Collegiality

In line with the Council's strong reaffirmation of the collegial character of the exercise of authority in the Church, the process of planning and composing the Catechism was a genuinely collegial effort on the part of all the bishops of the world in communion with the pope.

In response to the recommendation of the 1985 Synod of Bishops, our Holy Father appointed a commission of cardinals and bishops in 1986 to oversee the preparation of the new Catechism. The initial drafts of the Catechism were in fact developed by members of this commission, working with an international team of scholars.

By the close of 1989, the commission felt ready to circulate a draft for consultation among the bishops of the world. While the bishops greeted this draft with widespread general approval, many of them submitted suggested revisions. In fact, a special computer software program had to be designed in order to access and evaluate the more than 24,000 amendments submitted by the bishops!

When the commission finished its work on April 30, 1992, and our Holy Father approved it two months later, the new Catechism could truly be called a product of the entire worldwide episcopate exercising its collegial teaching authority in union with the Pope.

The Soul of the Catechism: Sacred Scripture

In addition to being a genuinely collegial document, the new Catechism heeds the Council's call for renewed reading and understanding of the Bible. The presentation of doctrine in the Catechism is thus profoundly scriptural. Even in a casual perusal of the Catechism, a reader cannot miss this striking feature of the text. The words of Scripture suffuse its account of the creed, the sacraments, the commandments, and the life of prayer. In effect an extended commentary on the Scripture, the Catechism teaches its readership to understand the "library" of the Old and New Testaments as a single book focused on Jesus Christ and the divine communion into which he initiates us.

Far from being a substitute for the Bible, the new Catechism is a gateway to its deepest meaning and continually invites the reader to savor it directly. It demonstrates that Catholics never read the Bible alone or in isolation from the community of faith and the great company of witnesses who through the centuries have pondered its meaning and unfolded its riches for others. If you imagine a Bible study group composed not just of your neighbors and friends, but of St. Augustine, St. Catherine of Siena, Pope John XXIII, and the fathers of Vatican II, you will not be far from grasping the nature of the Catholic way of reading the Bible. As the Catechism shows, an authentically Catholic reading of the Bible always sees the sacred text in the context of its liturgical, homiletical, exegetical, theological, magisterial, and doctrinal uses throughout Christian history. Following the lead of the Council, the Catechism continually invites the reader to turn to the Scriptures themselves and to meet Christ himself in the pages of these sacred books.

The Catechism's Recovery of the Sources of Tradition

In addition to encouraging a more profound study of the Scripture, the Second Vatican Council both called for and embodied a "return to the sources" (a *ressourcement*), a deepened rediscovery of the other great sources of the Catholic tradition, especially the liturgy, the Fathers of the Church, the statements of popes and councils, and the writings of the great saints and doctors.

At every point in its presentation of the faith, the Catechism expertly marshals these witnesses of the tradition to illumine, confirm, and explain Catholic dogmatic, sacramental, moral, and spiritual teachings. The reader of the Catechism meets not only the prophets and the evangelists, but also Pope St. Gregory the Great, St. John Damascene, St. Bonaventure, St. Teresa of Ávila, Cardinal Newman, St. Thérèse of Lisieux, and many others. The riches of the whole Catholic tradition unfold for the reader on every page of the new Catechism.

The Glory of the Faith

In its return to the sources, the Second Vatican Council was confident that, by recovering and presenting the most ancient and multifaceted witnesses to the Catholic tradition, the inherent attractiveness and power of the faith could be exhibited to the modern world.

Thus, although the Council was concerned with dialogue and apologetics, its presentation of the faith was remarkably unapologetic. It was declarative and direct. There was an underlying conviction, shared by many of the fathers of the Council and by leading theologians of the *ressourcement* movement, that the most persuasive case for the Christian faith could be made by a straightforward and non-apologetic presentation of its riches.

The Catechism is markedly conciliar in embodying this declarative, rather than apologetic, style of presentation. Within the limits of a single, fairly manageable book, the Catechism strives to present the fullness of the Catholic faith in a way that cannot fail to capture the attention and interest of believers and nonbelievers alike. No effort is made to mute the challenge or to dilute the richness of the evangelical call to transformation and communion in Christ. In this way, the Catechism serves an apologetical function without consciously striving to be apologetic about the faith and hope that is in us.

Ecumenical Dialogue

Again, in line with Vatican II, this feature of the Catechism makes it an important tool in dialogue with other Christians, with our Jewish brothers and sisters, with adherents of other religions, and with nonbelievers. The Catechism both expresses the spirit of ecumenical respect for other traditions of belief that was encouraged by the Council, and embodies the forthright presentation of the Catholic faith that such respect demands. In his encyclical *Ut unum sint*, our Holy Father reiterates this challenge. Dialogue requires of all its participants — Catholics no less than others — a fidelity to the distinctive teachings and ethos of their traditions.

Collegiality, biblical renewal, *ressourcement*, forthrightness in the presentation of the faith, ecumenical spirit — in each of these areas, the Catechism embodies the legacy of the Council and deserves to be called its catechism.

Chapter 3

Communion and Transformation

CATECHISM OF THE CATHOLIC CHURCH ¶26 - ¶100

When people talk about what matters most to them, they invariably mention other people — the husbands and wives, the sons and daughters, the mothers and fathers, and the friends whom they love. These fundamental personal relationships give human life its meaning.

Christians believe that the same thing is in a real sense true of God as well: When God speaks of what matters most to him, he speaks of the Father, Son, and Holy Spirit. The divine life is a life shared by three Persons who in turn want to share it with us.

Trinitarian Communion

As Pope John Paul II has said, we can never take for granted the "stunning novelty" of this truth about God and, by his grace, about ourselves that stands at the very center of our faith. Through the teaching and example of Christ, as the Catechism amply demonstrates, we have learned that what matters most to us matters most to God as well. God has revealed and the Church has faithfully proclaimed this great truth about his inner life. It is an uncreated interpersonal life shared by the Father, Son, and Holy Spirit, into which created persons have been invited and in which, through Christ, they can truly share. The One who created and sustains the universe dwells not in splendid isolation or in static self-possession but in the glory of interpersonal communion.

The Scriptures and the Liturgy of the Church have not hesitated to employ the language of family life to express this mystery and our participation in it. Jesus Christ, who is the Son by nature, makes it possible for us to be sons and daughters by adoption. In one of the Sunday prefaces, we pray that the Father will "see and love in us what [he sees and loves] in Christ."

The intimacy that we share in Christ with the Father, Son, and Holy Spirit entitles us, as it were, to use the private, proper, and "familial" names that the three Persons use in "addressing" each other. A passage from St. Cyprian's commentary on the Our Father makes this point vividly: "Let us pray as God our master has taught us. To ask the Father in words his Son has given us, to let him hear the prayer of Christ ringing in his ears, is to make our prayer one of friendship, a family prayer. Let the Father recognize the words of his Son. Let the Son who lives in our hearts be also on our lips."

This explains why the Church is not free to alter the language by which it addresses the Father, Son, and Holy Spirit. In sharing these names with us, Christ affords the most intimate personal access to the life of the Blessed Trinity. We are in no position to prefer other names, no matter how noble our purposes might be.

The Catechism frames its entire discussion of the Christian faith in terms of this trinitarian mystery as it is expressed in the threefold "*credo*" of the Profession of Faith: "I believe in God the Father almighty"; "I believe in Jesus Christ, the only Son of God"; "I believe in the Holy Spirit." All of the great mysteries of the Christian faith — creation, revelation, incarnation, redemption, communion, the Church, our Lady, and the last things — unfold in the Catechism as elements of the single mystery of the divine Trinity. In this way, it is made clear that the human words — "I believe" — are words on the lips of created persons who long for the perfect consummation of interpersonal life that the uncreated Persons enjoy and have undertaken to share with us.

The Catechism makes equally clear that the trinitarian mystery is for us a christological mystery and an ecclesial mystery as well.

Transformation in Christ and Communion in the Spirit

In the Incarnation, the divine Son took on human nature and became man in order to enable human persons to participate in the divine life. In the paschal mystery, Christ's perfect obedience atoned for the human disobedience and sin that would interfere with the enjoyment of this participation in the divine life. Christ's grace is thus a truly divinizing and reconciling grace that transforms, empowers, and heals human nature so that human persons can enjoy interpersonal life at a divine level. Christ is the principle and pattern of the transformation that constitutes our communion with the triune God.

By making us sons and daughters of the Father, Christ also makes us brothers and sisters. Our communion with the Father, Son, and Holy Spirit is also a communion with one another in them. Hence, the mystery at the heart of the Profession of Faith is at once trinitarian, christological, *and* ecclesial. Underlying the visible, worldwide communion of the Church as a public, social, and historical institution there is an invisible communion established by the Holy Spirit. The deepest bonds uniting the Church arise in the first place not in voluntary human undertakings or associations but from the divine initiative and grace. We were no people before we were God's people.

The Catechism structures its presentation of the truths of Christian faith around this trinitarian, Christological, and ecclesial core. All the elements of Christian belief, moral life, sacramental and liturgical practice, and spiritual theology have their meaning in relation to this fundamental core. The Catechism speaks of an "organic connection" among the elements of Christian belief and life. The source of this interrelation is Christ: "The mutual connections between dogmas, and their coherence, can be found in the whole of the Revelation of the mystery of Christ" (90; cf. Vatican Council I: DS 3016; *nexus mysteriorum*; LG, 25).

The Hierarchy of Truths

In making this point, the Catechism quotes a sentence from the documents of the Second Vatican Council: "In Catholic doctrine there exists an order or 'hierarchy' of truths, since they vary in their relation to the foundation of the Christian faith" (UR, 11).

The term "hierarchy of truths" is sometimes misunderstood to mean that some of the truths of the faith are essential while others are more marginal or even dispensable. On this misunderstanding, "hierarchy of truths" is taken to be a description of various levels of authority that attach to particular doctrines and thus to the degrees of adherence by which they must be accepted.

Some people have taken the notion of the hierarchy of truths as a justification for a selective or cafeteria-style Catholicism. Whether such a form of Catholicism is really possible in the end is an important question. But the hierarchy of truths cannot be invoked to legitimate this kind of selective Catholicism.

For, as Father Avery Dulles has pointed out, none of the instances of this expression in the documents of Vatican II refers "to the authority with which a doctrine is taught or to the kind of assent required" but "to the relations among revealed truths, some of which are regarded as more central or foundational, others as subordinate or derivative."

It is in this second sense that the *Catechism of the Catholic Church* testifies to the hierarchy among Catholic truths. By underscoring the trinitarian, Christological, and ecclesial core of the mystery at the heart of our faith, the Catechism invites us to see every element of Christian life in relation to this mystery.

A simple analogy will help us to see what is at stake here. From its extremities down to its inner core, the human body is made up of many parts. We have fingers, toes, ears, and noses, as well as hearts, brains, and other vital inner organs. We know that we could live without a left pinky, though we couldn't live without a heart or brain. Although hearts and brains are critical to the functioning of a living human body — and therefore are more important than ears and fingers — most of us are not prepared to part with even the smallest part of a finger or an ear unless our survival absolutely depended on it.

For all its inadequacies, this analogy brings us close to the meaning of the hierarchy of truths in the Catholic faith. Every element of the faith takes its meaning and force from the trinitarian, Christological, and ecclesial core at the center of divine revelation. While it is true that the doctrine of the Blessed Trinity is closer to the center of the Christian faith than, say, the doctrine that there are seven sacraments, it does not follow that the latter doctrine is dispensable. Rather, the hierarchy of truths teaches us to look for the deepest meaning of the doctrine of the sacraments in the central doctrine of the blessed Trinity.

In other words, according to the hierarchy of truths, we have never given an adequate account of a particular doctrine of faith or morals if we have not connected it with the overarching mystery of communion and transformation which the Apostles' Creed confesses. It is only in the light of this mystery that we can properly understand Christian sexual morality, for example, or the Christian doctrine of creation, or the sacraments, or Mariology.

The Catechism not only makes this point vividly clear, it actually helps us both to understand and to teach the various elements of our faith within the context of an all-embracing vision of the whole of our faith. Whenever we try to understand or teach about a particular topic — whether it be a matter of faith or morals, liturgy or prayer — we must always ask ourselves how it fits in with the great mysteries of the blessed Trinity, of the Incarnation, passion, death, and resurrection of Christ, and of the communion of the Holy Spirit in the Church. This is the meaning of the hierarchy, or order, of Catholic truths.

The Communion of Love

It follows that teaching rightly and without error — what we have come to call "orthodoxy" — is not an end in itself. We want our faith to be complete and error-free because we want to be clear about the high destiny to which we are called and which we have already begun to live through Baptism. God the Father, Son, and Holy Spirit have opened their divine heart to us and have called out to us in love. Orthodoxy is meant to insure that we avoid any drastic mistakes or misunderstandings of what the triune God has revealed to us. The charism of the magisterium embodies Christ's irrevocable promise that the Church will never be led into error in these matters. It is for this reason that the Catechism can play such an important role in our life of faith: it seeks to capture within the covers of one book the personal knowledge we need to hear the voice of Christ calling to us, and to respond in love. Our faith rests not only in the doctrines in which it is expressed: through them, it leads our minds and hearts to God himself.

Nothing less than communion with the Father, Son, and Holy Spirit, and with one another in them, is the final destiny that God wills for human persons in Christ. And so, it turns out that what matters most to most of us is what matters most to the triune God: the communion of shared, interpersonal life. When the Catechism speaks of what matters most to Christians, it speaks chiefly about this mystery of the inner life of triune God and our destiny to share in it. St. Irenaeus expressed this deep Christian conviction with characteristic directness when he wrote that the triune God "who stands in need of no one gave communion with himself to those who need him." The new Catechism testifies to this conviction eloquently and extensively.

Chapter 4

The Triune God Draws Near

CATECHISM OF THE CATHOLIC CHURCH ¶1 - ¶25

The Catechism begins not with our search for God but with God's drawing close to us. This is the properly Christian starting point for all talk about God.

God's Search for Man

The first paragraph of the Prologue to the Catechism states this forthrightly: "God, infinitely perfect and blessed in himself, in a plan of sheer goodness freely created man to make him share his own blessed life. For this reason, at every time and place, God draws close to man. . . . In his Son and through him, he invites men to become, in the Holy Spirit, his adopted children and thus heirs of his blessed life" (1).

In this way, the Catechism is refreshingly "unmodern." No hint here of typically modern anxieties about God's absence, or about the human search for him. Without underestimating the significance of modern atheism and agnosticism, the Catechism refuses to allow these broad cultural movements to shape its account of the doctrine of God. Far from being absent, distant, or unengaged, God is closer to us than we are to ourselves.

The One who created the universe is immediately and continually present to every creature as First Cause. Over and beyond this sustaining presence, God freely makes himself the object of human personal knowledge and love through revelation and through the infused theological virtues of faith, hope, and charity. Surpassing even this presence is the hypostatic union, in which God joins a human nature to the Person of his Son. Short of the beatific vision itself, God could not be more present to human beings than he has undertaken to be in the Incarnation and in sanctifying grace.

Because of the unity of God's purposes in creation and redemption, our knowledge of the world which God has caused to exist can and should lead us to a knowledge of God. For this reason, we can draw upon science and philosophy as we strive to articulate the doctrine of God. But philosophical and scientific knowledge are embraced by the personal knowledge that comes through revelation and faith. A complete theology of God weaves together strands drawn both from revelation and from so-called "natural" knowledge.

Thus, as the first section of Part One of the Catechism makes clear, the Christian believer is never simply in the position of an expectant seeker who hopes for a signal or a word from that silent, and possibly impersonal, Presence, which surrounds and transcends the world, and to which the world bears faint witness. Rather, the believing community of the Church rejoices in the knowledge of a God who is all-consuming love and who, through grace and revelation, presses continually at the edges and in the depths of human knowledge and awareness.

These convictions of faith frame the properly Christian exposition of the doctrine of God that we find in the Catechism's approach to first article of the Apostles' Creed, "I believe in God the Father almighty, creator of heaven and earth." It begins, not with the typically modern quandary about how human beings can know God or speak about him, but with the deep Christian conviction that, in the first place, it is we who are known by God (see Gal 4:8-9), and that the words by which to speak of him are the words provided to us by revelation itself.

Our Knowledge of God

To be sure, the structures of human existence and experience are not irrelevant or alien to God's action in revelation and grace. On the contrary, human nature is so constituted by the Creator as to be "capable" precisely of the kind of transforming relationship that grace involves. As the Catechism puts it, "The desire for God is written in the human heart, because man is created by God and for God; and God never ceases to draw man to himself" (27). Human spiritual capacities are neither suppressed by revelation nor irrelevant to its forms of expression.

But our knowing of and speaking about God are now definitively shaped by the revelation of Christ. From Christ and through the Apostles we know that the God who created the world shares the divine life in a communion of Persons, Father, Son, and Holy Spirit. As the Catechism makes clear, this revelation was the culmination of a prolonged divine pedagogy that began with our first parents and unfolded in stages from Noah, through Abraham, and in the covenant with Israel. Christ is the climax of this revelation, and no further revelation will surpass the fullness we have received through him.

In making this point, the Catechism quotes a striking passage from St. John of the Cross: "In giving us his Son, his only Word (for he possesses no other), he spoke everything to us at once in this sole Word — and he has no more to say . . . because what he spoke before to the prophets in parts, he has now spoken all at once by giving us the All Who is His Son. Any person questioning God or desiring some vision or revelation would be guilty not only of foolish behavior but also of offending him, by not fixing his eyes entirely upon Christ and by living with the desire for some other novelty" (65).

This revelation forms the substance of the apostolic tradition, transmitted to us in the distinct modes of Scripture and tradition, and unendingly pondered and faithfully proclaimed by the magisterium. It is a revelation that nonetheless comes to us from God himself. For this reason, it forms the basis for a truly personal knowledge and initiates the interpersonal communion of love with the three-personed God that is our destiny in grace.

The Love That Never Ends

The Catechism's telling quotation of a passage from the Roman Catechism may be taken as defining the context for its exposition of the first article of the Apostles' Creed: "The whole concern of doctrine and its teaching must be directed to the love that never ends. Whether something is proposed for belief, for hope or for action, the love of our Lord must always be made accessible. . ." (25; Roman Catechism, Preface, 10; cf. I Cor 13:8). Everything that is embraced by the first article of the creed — "I believe in God the Father almighty, creator of heaven and earth" — must be understood with this "pastoral principle" in mind: faith in the one God; the doctrine of the Trinity; creation; angels; man and the visible world; the fall.

In a plan of sheer, superabundant love and for the manifestation of his glory, God created things visible and invisible in order to share his blessed life with the angels and us. The three-personed God who is one God opened the communion of the uncreated Persons to the intimate participation of created persons. The objective of divine providence is the consummation of this plan.

The Catechism teaches that the creation of man in God's image establishes the basis for the unfolding of this divine economy. Human persons are beings whose nature is fulfilled in knowing and loving other persons, and, above all, in knowing and loving God. This is what it means to say that we are made in the image of God. From the beginning of creation, God furnishes the transforming grace that empowers these natural capacities of knowing and loving to operate at a new level in knowing and loving God. Divine grace, from the beginning, enables human persons freely to embrace the divine offer of communion. Even the human failure to return this love — in the original sin of our first parents and its continuing impact on us, and in the many personal sins that we commit — cannot finally divert or thwart God's irrevocable resolve to share his divine life with creaturely persons.

Human beings, especially in modern times, have been preoccupied with the "search" for God and with the "problem" of God. Without denying or underestimating the significance of this preoccupation, the Christian cannot fail to be struck by the irony here. We do not have to search for a God who draws close to us, or agonize over the right words to describe and address a God who pursues us. As the Catechism makes clear in its entirety, we have but to turn to him, "God the Father almighty, creator of heaven and earth," and to listen to his Word to know all, and more than all, that we need to know about him. When we do turn to him, we might well do so with the words of the poet John Donne on our lips: "Batter my heart, o three-person'd God."

Chapter 5

At the Heart of Catechesis: Christ

CATECHISM OF THE CATHOLIC CHURCH ¶422 - ¶682

It is sometimes said that the four Gospels can be read as passion narratives with long introductions. There is a deep truth in this remark.

Only with the end of the story — only with the narrative of his passion, death, and resurrection — can the meaning of the rest of the story of Christ's earthly life and ministry be discerned: with perfect obedience to the Father's will Christ embraces the cross for our sake and thus removes the guilt of our disobedience. It is only from the perspective of this culminating mystery that we can penetrate the other mysteries of Christ's life and share in their benefits.

The Paschal Mystery

Here, our experience replicates that of the apostles, who were taught by the risen Christ to consider everything — not only in his earthly life, but in the entire previous history of salvation — in the light of the Paschal Mystery. After appearing to the apostles in the upper room, "he said to them: 'These are my words that I spoke to you while I was still with you, that everything written about me in the law of Moses and in the prophets and psalms must be fulfilled.' Then he opened their minds to understand the scriptures. And he said to them, 'Thus it is written that the Messiah would suffer and rise from the dead on the third day' " (Lk 24:44-46).

The Catechism makes it clear that, like the apostles, we come to an understanding of the mysteries of Christ's life, and indeed even share in them, only through the lens of the mystery of his passion, death, resurrection, and glory. Indeed, the Catechism asserts, this mystery is "at the heart of catechesis" where "we find, in essence, a Person, the Person of Jesus of Nazareth, the only Son of the Father . . . who suffered and died for us and who now, after rising, is living with us forever" (426; CT, 5).

Following the order of the Creed's affirmations about Christ, the Catechism takes up in turn his proper names and titles, the Incarnation, the grace of Mary's *fiat*, the mysteries of his hidden and public life, his proclamation of the kingdom of God, his passion and death, his descent into hell, his resurrection and ascension, his glorious reign and awaited return as Judge of the living and the dead. Each of these affirmations centers on the culminating act of perfect obedience that restores humankind to fellowship with God.

The Incarnation

"Christ was born for this," sings the familiar Christmas carol, "In Dulci Jubilo":

He has opened heaven's door,
And man is blessed evermore,
Christ was born for this.

Christ was born for this. The Incarnation — the coming of the only Son of God as man — was for this. Only Jesus Christ, who is inseparably true God and true man, can restore us to friendship with God. The Catechism quotes St. Irenaeus: "For this is why the Word became man, and the Son of God became the Son of man: so that man, by entering into communion with the Word and thus receiving divine sonship, might become a son of God" (460).

It is neither ironic nor inappropriate that the great feast of the Annunciation should fall every year within the season of Lent. In consenting to the angel's message that she was to be the mother of "the Son of the Most High," Mary in effect embraced the divine will for our salvation in its totality. Her readiness to embrace this will is itself the result of the absolute divine initiative that "prepares the way" for the coming of the Son both in Mary's Immaculate Conception and in her virginal motherhood. The grace of her Immaculate Conception shows that she is indeed the first fruits of Christ's redemptive death: Mary is preserved from sin in virtue of the cross of her Son. The grace of her perpetual virginity shows that it is God alone who is the Father of Jesus: Mary's motherhood is the work of the Holy Spirit. The Catechism draws the connection between the Annunciation of Mary and the redemptive obedience of Christ in an explicit way by quoting some striking words of St. Irenaeus: "Being obedient she became the cause of salvation for herself and for the whole human race" (494).

The Mysteries of Christ's Life and the Paschal Mystery

While the Catechism admits that the Creed is silent on the subject of the mysteries of Christ's earthly life and teaching, it nonetheless affirms that "the articles of faith concerning his Incarnation and Passover do shed light on the *whole* of his earthly life" (512). Between Christmas and Easter, every moment of Christ's life was lived for us. Again, St. Irenaeus has just the right words: "Christ experienced all the stages of life, thereby giving communion with God to all men" (518). In every stage of Christ's life, the mystery of our redemption was manifested: in the self-emptying of the Incarnation, in his obedient submission to human parents, and in his teaching and miracles which healed and purified his listeners.

Christ's infancy, his hidden life, his baptism by John, his temptation in the desert, his proclamation of the kingdom, and his Transfiguration — each of these moments moved him inexorably towards the obedient embrace of his Father's will. The Catechism quotes Pope John Paul II to this effect: "The whole of Christ's life was a continual teaching: his silences, his miracles, his gestures, his prayer, his love for people, his special affection for the little and the poor, his acceptance of the total sacrifice on the Cross for the redemption of the world, and his Resurrection are the actualization of his Word and the fulfillment of Revelation" (561).

Christ's Passion, Death, and Resurrection

The gospels make it quite clear that Christ set his face toward Jerusalem with deliberation and determination. It was the obedience with which he embraced the cross that was finally decisive in bringing about our salvation. His death to sin, his apparent defeat by the devil, would be revealed as a definitive victory over death and sin in his resurrection.

It is a striking feature of the passion narratives that no one "character" can by himself be blamed for what happens to Christ. None of the dramatis personae, acting alone, could have brought Jesus to the cross. Rather, it is a conspiracy of sin and sinners that bring about his death: the envy of some of the religious leadership, the cowardice of some of the apostles and disciples, the betrayal of Judas, the venality of Herod, the weakness and vacillation of Pilate, the mass hysteria of the crowd, the cruelty of the soldiers, and so on. In this way, Jesus literally succumbs not just to one kind of sin, but to all sins. Thus, his resurrection can be seen as a victory over all sins and for all sinners. Because all are implicated in the sins, all are embraced in the prayer of forgiveness which he utters from the cross.

It is for this reason, as the Catechism makes clear in its discussion of the Jewish people, that no one group can be blamed for the crucifixion of Christ. For, ironically, to assign blame for his crucifixion and death to any one group is, in effect, precisely to *exclude* oneself from its benefits.

Only when one, through confession and repentance, takes responsibility for bringing Christ to the cross can one share in its victory. The sin of blaming the Jews is not just one of injustice against them; it is a sin of unrepentance which hurts the offending Christian in the very core of his own spirit.

Thus, when, during the commemoration of Christ's passion on Good Friday, the congregation utters the seemingly terrible words, "Let his blood be upon us and upon our children," the Church is affirming its faith that only by being washed in the blood of Christ can we be freed from sin and restored to friendship with God.

On Easter Sunday, when we gaze upon the risen Christ, we know that it was for *our* sins that he died and that it was *our* sins that he defeated. We know that no sins, however great, are more powerful than the power of Christ who vanquished them.

Now Christ sits at the right hand of the Father, and we await his coming in glory as Judge. The expectation of Christ's judgment should not be a terrifying prospect for us, but a liberating one. He who is victorious over sin is the only true judge. He frees us from the burden of judging others and of judging ourselves.

As the Catechism makes clear, our own entry into the mysteries of Christ's life demands that we view everything between Christmas and the Second Coming in the light of the glory that blazes from the face of the crucified and risen Son of God.

Chapter 6

Communion in the Holy Spirit

CATECHISM OF THE CATHOLIC CHURCH ¶683 - ¶780

The Church is God's creation. This is a truth we can easily forget.

The Church of God

So much of the Church's day-to-day life depends on us: our attendance, response, support, devotion, readiness to volunteer. We forget that there is a Church only because God has gathered a chosen people to himself. We forget that we are part of this Church only because we have been claimed by Christ and baptized in the Holy Spirit. The foundation for the visible communion of the Church is the invisible communion with the Father, Son, and Holy Spirit which is God's gift to us and which sanctifying grace makes possible. The Catechism states that the Church is the sacrament of this trinitarian communion.

Several factors conspire to produce a practical forgetfulness of this fundamental truth of our Catholic faith. Our participation in the Church's life seems more or less to parallel other kinds of participation in voluntary and professional associations. In a variety of clubs, fraternities, unions, alliances, and societies, we join with other like-minded people who share our social background, interests, and goals.

Americans are great joiners. For many of us, the Church is just another organization we decided to join and support. This way of thinking is abetted by the typically American penchant for forming new denominations and church communities. Our "religious affiliation" is just one more item in our personal profiles.

While it is true that our belonging to the Church entails a free act — it must if it is to be truly personal — it is also true that this is a *divinely enabled* free act that brings us a share in a communion with the triune God and with each other in him that is a *divine gift*. Our membership and participation in the Church is already a membership in the divine "family" of the uncreated Persons and a participation in the divine life.

In the Catholic understanding, expounded by the Catechism, the formation of the Church is in the first place a divine initiative and action. We have become part of something that preexists our interests, determinations, plans, and objectives: we have become partakers of the divine life. In Baptism, we have become part of a hierarchically constituted community of persons that flows from God and rests in him. As God in effect announced to Israel after the Exodus from Egypt: "you were no people before you were my people."

Catholic tradition associates the Holy Spirit in a particular way with this divine constitution of the Church.

The Sacrament of Trinitarian Communion

Properly understood, of course, it is the joint mission of Christ and his Spirit that establishes the communion of the Church. As the Catechism strikingly affirms, the Church's mission is "not an addition to that of Christ and the Holy Spirit, but it is its sacrament" (738).

The Church is thus the Body of Christ and the Temple of the Holy Spirit. "For just as the power of Christ's sacred flesh unites those in whom it dwells into one body," wrote St. Cyril of Alexandria, "in the same way the one and undivided Spirit of God, who dwells in all, leads all into spiritual unity" (738).

The Church's faith in God is a faith in the triune God revealed to us by Christ and fully manifested on the day of Pentecost. The Father, Son, and Holy Spirit are equally, consubstantially, and inseparably one God, yet distinct in their relations. By the gracious and loving design of this triune God, created persons are destined to share in the communion of life that properly belongs to the uncreated Persons. In a deeply mysterious way, the Church's life reflects the life of the blessed Trinity, and indeed is a foretaste of that life.

Communion in the Holy Spirit

It is especially the grace of Pentecost and the work of the Holy Spirit "to awaken faith in us and to communicate to us the new life, which is to 'know the Father and the one whom he has sent, Jesus Christ' (684; Jn 17:3)." This new life constitutes the bond that unites the Church. Since it is the particular mission of the Holy Spirit to preserve and nourish this life, the Church traditionally appropriates the following graces to the Holy Spirit: He inspired Scripture, preserves the tradition, assists the magisterium, puts us into communion with Christ in the sacred liturgy, intercedes for us in prayer, builds up the Church through special charisms, and manifests his holiness in the lives of the saints.

Underscoring its fundamentally trinitarian character, St. Irenaeus summarized this multifaceted grace of the Holy Spirit when he wrote: "It is impossible to see God's Son without the Spirit, and no one can approach the Father without the Son, for the knowledge of the Father is the Son, and the knowledge of God's Son is obtained through the Holy Spirit" (683).

The Church: Human and Divine

The very word "church" embodies the truth of its divine constitution. The Latin term *ecclesia* (based on the Greek) refers to God's "calling a people together" before him, while the English term "church" (based on the German word *Kirche*) means "what belongs to God." These terms reflect the truth that the Church rests in the first place on the divine initiative and grace. The Catechism quotes Vatican II's *Lumen gentium* to this effect: "The Father . . . determined to call together in a holy Church those who should believe in Christ" (759).

At the same time, as the Catechism makes clear, the Church is a human institution — visible, socially organized, and hierarchically structured. The divine grace that is the foundation of the Church's invisible life is a grace given to human persons. For this reason, it is at once divinely constituted and socially organized. Once again, the Catechism quotes *Lumen gentium*: "The one mediator, Christ, established and ever sustains here on earth his holy Church, the community of faith, hope and charity, as a visible organization through which he communicates truth and grace to all men" (771).

The Catechism identifies this double constitution as the "mystery" of the Church. She is both visible and spiritual, the very setting of the union between human persons and the triune God, and the very sign of this sacred union to the world. According to *Lumen gentium*: "The Church, in Christ, is in the nature of a sacrament — a sign and instrument . . . of communion with God and of unity among all men" (775; LG, 1).

Throughout its discussion of the marks of the Church — one, holy, catholic, and apostolic — the Catechism keeps this fundamental mystery of the Church's reality always in sight. Every aspect of the Church's life and mission must be seen in connection with the underlying mystery of trinitarian communion to which the Church bears concrete witness. Christ instituted the ecclesial ministry of the Church in all its levels with a view precisely to the faith service of this mystery for the salvation of all.

Nothing makes clearer the divine origin and destiny of the Church than the confession of faith in the communion of saints, and in the mystery of Mary's motherhood of God and of the Church. Our communion with the holy ones who have gone before us — both those who are still being purified and those who now share the unmediated vision of the triune God — reveals the true goal of our earthly pilgrimage. Just as Mary brought the Redeemer into the world, so does she "mother" the Church in grace, through her intercession and example.

Chapter 7

Christ, First and Last

CATECHISM OF THE CATHOLIC CHURCH ¶988 - ¶1060

The years surrounding the close of the second millennium and the start of the third are likely to arouse a range of bizarre expectations and nameless anxieties. It is a time when the serene voice of authentic Catholic faith about the first *and* the last things will need to be heard.

Communion at the End and at the Beginning

The Catechism teaches us that the last things can only be understood in the perspective of the first. The end of the world, and of each particular human life, must be seen as the consummation of the divine plan to save us through the Incarnation, passion, death, and resurrection of Christ. First and last, the divine invitation to embrace communion with the Father, Son, and Holy Spirit, and with one another in them, frames and suffuses human history from the beginning to the end of the time. Resurrection of the body, life everlasting, particular judgment, heaven, purgatory, hell, last judgment, and the hope of a new heaven and a new earth, each of these elements in the Catholic doctrine of the last things must be viewed in the light of the invitation to trinitarian communion that comes to us through Christ.

Trinitarian communion is *personal* communion. In grace, created persons are drawn into the communion of the uncreated Persons of the Father, Son, and Holy Spirit. It is fundamental to the consummation of the divine plan that we continue in eternal life as the identifiable, albeit transfigured and glorified, persons we are now. The significance of the doctrine of the resurrection of the body lies here.

Personal Destiny: Resurrection and Immortality

Our personhood is constituted by an essential unity of body and soul. Contrary to what sometimes masquerades as Christian thought on these matters, the body is not an accidental or disposable appurtenance to the real personal identity located in the soul. Our bodiliness is essential to the identity of the persons we are. For this reason, the Catholic doctrine about the life to come can never be expressed solely in terms of the immortality of the soul, but must always include the resurrection of the body. For this reason, as well, the notions of the reincarnation of souls in human and subhuman forms, and of the divine absorption of souls, must be judged to be utterly alien to authentic Christian faith.

The Catechism states this clearly. The everlasting life made possible for us through Christ's conquest of death in his own resurrection is the continued, though transformed, life of embodied persons who, precisely as persons, will enjoy communion with the divine Persons of the blessed Trinity and with one another in them.

The other central elements in the Catholic doctrine of the last things — death, particular judgment, heaven, purgatory, and hell — must also be placed in trinitarian perspective.

Heaven

Life in Christ is life lived in view of the fullness of trinitarian communion. As our Holy Father taught in *Veritatis splendor* and the Catechism clearly states in its treatment of the beatitudes and commandments in Part Three, the moral life is our divinely enabled, free embrace of the ultimate Good of trinitarian communion. In a growing conformity to Christ, according to the pattern of his passion, death, and resurrection, our struggle to choose the good in every occasion of action and in extended patterns of action contributes to our developing fitness for the enjoyment of this trinitarian communion.

According to the Catechism, heaven is the "perfect life with the Most Holy Trinity," the "communion of life and love with the Trinity, with the Virgin Mary, the angels and all the blessed" (1024). It can be enjoyed only by those who are "perfectly purified." This language is important, particularly in order to correct the idea that heaven is an extrinsic reward conferred for the successful completion of the arduous obstacle-course that is human life on earth. Moral life and purification — life in Christ — render the Christian *fit to enjoy* the glorified life of trinitarian communion in heaven.

Hell

But a life of mortal sin and persistent unrepentance could render a person permanently *unfit* for the enjoyment of this communion. If this condition perdures to the point of death and beyond — if, in the words of the Catechism, a person by his own free choice dies "in mortal sin without repenting and accepting God's merciful love" (1033) — then he remains separated from him forever. God neither predestines nor consigns anyone to hell. Rather, hell is the natural consequence of a life lived apart from God. The terrible suffering of hell consists in the realization that, over the course of a lifetime, one has come, not to love, but to hate one's true good, and thus to be radically unfit to enjoy that Good.

It is this pain of loss that is central to the Catholic understanding of hell. Imagine the predicament of one who both knows that God is the great love of his life, and that he has turned irreversibly away from this love. This is what hell is.

Purgatory

Since no one who is not fit can actually enjoy the ultimate good of trinitarian communion, the Catechism teaches that all "who die in God's grace and friendship, but still imperfectly purified, are indeed assured of their eternal salvation . . . but after death they undergo purification, so as to achieve the holiness necessary to enter the joy of heaven" (1030). According to Catholic tradition, God has provided for this interval of further purification in purgatory.

Consider an analogy. Suppose that you are standing at your window watching a group of your friends pile into a van on their way to play tennis. You want very much to be with them, but you know that your game just isn't good enough yet. Still, you are certain that, with the regular lessons you have been taking, you will soon be able to join your friends on the court. The Saturday morning will come when you are ready for an enjoyment that, for the moment, must be deferred.

In effect, purgatory is a temporarily deferred enjoyment of promised bliss. The souls in purgatory — whom, St. John Chrysostom says, we must "not hesitate to help" with our prayers (1032) — are assured of the bliss of full trinitarian communion but know that they must be completely purified in order to enjoy it.

The Last Judgment

According to the Catechism, the doctrine of the particular judgment affirms that only Christ can determine each man's fitness at the very moment of death to enter into heaven through a purification or immediately or into everlasting damnation (see 1022). The doctrine of the last, or general, judgment, on the other hand, affirms our faith that, with Christ's return in glory, "the good each person has done or failed to do during his earthly life" (1039) will be revealed, as well as the "ultimate meaning of the whole work of creation and of the entire economy of salvation," and "the marvelous ways by which [God's] Providence led everything towards its final end" (1040).

The end of time, then, is not just an ending but a consummation. The world, and human beings with it, do not simply come to an end. They rather reach the end, arrive at the goal, for which God created all things.

Towards the end of its treatment of the last things, the Catechism tellingly quotes Vatican II's *Gaudium et spes*: "We know neither the moment of the consummation of the earth and of man, nor the way in which the universe will be transformed. The form of this world, distorted by sin, is passing away, and we are taught that God is preparing a new dwelling and a new earth in which righteousness dwells, in which happiness will fill and surpass all the desires of peace arising in the hearts of men" (1048; GS, 39).

Thus it is that, for the Christian, anxiety yields to faith, hope, and love as the transition to the new millennium is marked, not by fear and suspense, but by celebration and thanksgiving. As Pope John Paul II stated in his recent apostolic letter on preparation for the year 2000 (*Tertio millennio adveniente*), this is a time "to confirm the Christians of today in their *faith* in God who has revealed himself in Christ, sustain their *hope* which reaches out in expectation of eternal life, and rekindle their *charity* in active service to their brothers and sisters."

From first to last, from the beginning of time to its end, all is embraced in the great mystery of trinitarian communion revealed to us by Christ — the communion of "true and subsistent life," in the words of St. Gregory the Great, "the Father, through the Son and in the Holy Spirit, pouring out his gifts on all things without exception."

Chapter 8

The Celebration of the Christian Mystery

CATECHISM OF THE CATHOLIC CHURCH ¶1066 - ¶1112

God's relentless search for man as recounted in Part One of the Catechism is at the heart of all talk about God. In the same way, God's initiative in drawing close to us and providing all the means required for us to reciprocate, for us to draw close to God, is at the heart of Part Two of the Catechism.

Liturgy and Sacraments

The liturgy and the sacraments are the central ways in which God continues the work of Christ in the Church. These moments of worship and sacrament effect that transformation which is necessary if we are to realize our destiny: ultimate communion with the God who is a community of love, the Father, Son, and Holy Spirit.

By "liturgy" the Catechism means God's saving action toward us in Christ, the "mystery of his will," and our response to God in Christ. Rooted in God's initiative and action, the liturgy is at one and the same time our praise, thanksgiving, and adoration for what God has done for us *and* the presence of that saving action again through the mystery of Jesus Christ. "The dual dimension of the Christian liturgy as a response of faith and love to the spiritual blessings the Father bestows on us" (1083) is perfectly expressed in the mystery of the Incarnation of Christ. Jesus Christ is at the center of the liturgy. As both God and man he is God's perfect gift to us and our perfect response to that gift. At the heart of the liturgy are the sacraments, the ways in which Christ continues to be present and effective among his people. Thus the Catechism often refers to the "sacramental liturgy" of the Church.

The Liturgy and the Paschal Mystery

The central motif of Part Two of the Catechism is that of the Paschal Mystery of Jesus Christ, his passion, death, and resurrection, as it is celebrated in the liturgy and continues to be effective *for* us and *within* us in the sacraments. The passion, death, and resurrection of Jesus Christ is not only an historical event which accomplished our salvation and offered acceptable worship to God, an event like other historical events that happen once and then is swallowed up in the past. The Paschal Mystery of Christ cannot remain only in the past since what Christ accomplished through his cross, indeed all that he is as the Christ, participates in the divine eternity and thereby transcends the category of time even while being made present within it. The victory over death and the consecration of all suffering continues to exist in the glorified humanity of Christ *now* seated at the right hand of the Father. "The event of the Cross and Resurrection *abides* and draws everything toward life" (1085).

This central theme of the Paschal Mystery links Part Two with the other parts of the Catechism, the other "pillars," on which the whole structure of the Catechism rests. In Part One we learn that the "Paschal Mystery of Christ's cross and resurrection stands at the center of the Good News" (571). In Part Three, concerning Christian moral life, we learn that Christians "are called to lead . . . a life 'worthy of the gospel of Christ,' . . . made capable of doing so by the grace of Christ and the gifts of his Spirit, which they receive through the sacraments and through prayer" (1692; Phil 1:27). Finally, Part Four in exploring prayer and the spiritual life tells us that "prayer internalizes and assimilates the liturgy during and after its celebration" (2655).

In this way, each of the distinct parts of the Catechism are closely related to one another. Precisely because worship and sacraments are the common public actions in which all Catholics must of necessity be involved, there is a sense in which Part Two is *the* integrating principle of the whole Catechism. The Second Vatican Council expressed this forcefully by declaring that the liturgy is "the source and summit" of all of the Church's activity.

Participation in the Communion of the Blessed Trinity

While Part One of the Catechism reveals the centrality of the mystery of Christ in his passion, death, and resurrection, Part Two, the Paschal Mystery, sets this central theme within the broader context of trinitarian life.

This is one of the distinctive characteristics of the Catechism: again and again, it leads us back to the unifying principle of God's self-revelation as a Trinity of persons, Father, Son, and Holy Spirit. In a mood at once mystical and yet within our grasp, Part Two situates the Paschal Mystery within the context of the "plan of the mystery," that is, God's plan for the salvation of the world through the sending of his beloved Son and the Holy Spirit.

God reveals himself not only as a community of trinitarian love, but also as one whose love "overflows" into his work of creation, redemption, and the invitation to ultimate communion, the invitation to participate in the very community of love which is God's own life. In its liturgy and the sacraments, the Church celebrates the Paschal Mystery of Christ's "Passion, Resurrection from the dead, and glorious Ascension" (1067) as a manifestation of God's true nature, an expression of God's initiative in sharing his life with us, and our response of praise and thanksgiving. Through the liturgy and the sacraments, God accomplishes what he has promised: our transformation in Christ. Only in this way can we be made ready for our life of communion with him and with each other in him for all eternity.

It follows that the Catechism strongly emphasizes the role of the Holy Spirit in the trinitarian "work" of the Church's liturgy and sacraments. The mystical "mood" of Part Two is intensified through a theological accent reminiscent of the Eastern Church when the Catechism consistently returns to the central role of the Holy Spirit in accomplishing the ongoing celebration of the Paschal Mystery. Just as the Father sends the Son into the world for its salvation, the Son now sends the Holy Spirit into the world to prepare the Church for the reality of his Paschal Mystery, to make it present, and to effect in each Christian that grace which flows from the side of the crucified Christ now risen and glorious. This is the grace of the sacraments, the grace of the sacred humanity of Christ now made present and effective by the Spirit in the liturgy and sacraments of the Church.

Note the language of the Catechism in speaking of the role of the Spirit in sacraments: terms such as power, energy, action, teaching, transforming, designing and fulfilling, when used in reference to the Spirit, reveal a theological breadth and depth which considerably enhance the Catechism's versatility and appeal.

The Catechism is careful to show how the sacramental liturgy of the Church has a special relationship to each person of the Trinity. The Father is acknowledged as the source and goal of the liturgy. He fills us with his blessings and "pours into our hearts the Gift that contains all gifts, the Holy Spirit" (1082). The liturgy and the sacraments are the work of the Son, Jesus Christ, who is both priest and victim, for it is his Paschal Mystery which he signifies and makes present in the liturgy. The Holy Spirit prepares the Church for the reception of Christ and makes the mystery of Christ present in the sacramental liturgy of the Church. This trinitarian action is accomplished in order to bring us into communion with Christ: sacramental communion here on earth in the liturgy and ultimate communion with him in heaven.

It is dramatic indeed to realize that we are the object of God's desire and design. Each day the Church continues to reveal this desire and plan of God in its sacramental liturgy.

Chapter 9

The Sacramental Economy

CATECHISM OF THE CATHOLIC CHURCH ¶1113 - ¶1162

Through the prophet Isaiah the Lord warns: "My thoughts are not your thoughts, nor are your ways my ways" (Is 55:8). Clearly God is totally "other" than creatures, including man who is made in his image and likeness. The prophet never claims, however, that we cannot know God's thoughts and ways. Indeed, in the whole of revelation, God tells of his choices and actions.

The liturgy is one of the privileged moments in which we have access to God's thoughts and desires. In the celebration of the Paschal Mystery God tells us over and over again that he *is* thinking about us and about our world, and he shares with us the content of these thoughts and desires, our salvation in Jesus Christ. In the sacraments, God's "ways" are manifest, for in the sacraments he acts on his thoughts "for us men and for our salvation," as the Creed puts it.

God's Thoughts and Ways

The wonder of the liturgy and the sacraments is that they give us access to God's thoughts and God's ways. Aside from the sacraments of the Church, we know of no other way in which God himself has undertaken to communicate his own life and the mystery of his love. It is not that God is confined to the liturgy and the sacraments. Certainly they do not exhaust his activity nor his power of self-communication. Rather, the sacramental liturgy of the Church is the way which *God* has designed and he wills all men and women to use them in order to come to know him, to love him, and to serve him.

The sacramental liturgy of the Church is God's *way* of realizing the invitation to ultimate communion, the progressive movement into the heart of the Church and into the heart of God himself. Hence, borrowing a phrase from the ancient tradition, the Catechism describes the whole economy of salvation as "the sacramental economy."

At Pentecost, God manifested his thoughts most dramatically through the sending of the Holy Spirit upon the apostles and disciples. He established the "age of the Church" in which Christ "manifests, makes present and communicates his work of salvation through the liturgy of his Church" (1076). The fruits of the Paschal Mystery come to us through the sacraments. This point is critical for a proper understanding of the structure and content of Part Two of the Catechism, which begins with an exploration of the notions of liturgy and sacraments.

Building on this central theme of the Paschal Mystery of Christ and a consideration of the nature of the liturgy of the Church, the Catechism enlarges our theological horizons through a clear exposition of the relationship between the Church's liturgy and the Trinity, and through a consideration of the nature and significance of the sacraments. Just as the liturgy in its entirety is rooted in the Trinity, the sacraments are, in a particular way, the work of Jesus Christ.

Christ in the Sacraments

In reflecting on the sacraments, our starting point must be the mystery of the Incarnation: Jesus Christ, the second Person of the blessed Trinity, became man. When the Catechism declares that the sacraments are the work of Christ, it means that the sacred humanity of Christ in his hidden and public life, the mysteries of his life on earth, are the foundations of what he continues to communicate to us in the sacraments of the Church. In the Incarnation, not only does God "stoop down" to take on a human nature. At the same time, he "lifts up" human nature to a new possibility — a share in divine life. The sacraments are about this "marvelous exchange."

The Catechism quotes Pope St. Leo the Great's explanation: "What was visible in our Savior has passed over into his mysteries" (1115). The sacraments are the powers which come forth from the body of Christ, now risen and glorious. All sacraments and all sacramental grace come to us from the sacred glorified humanity of Christ.

Exactly what "unleashes" these powers from the side of Christ?

The liturgy. The words and actions of the Church call upon the Father to send forth once again the Holy Spirit in order to communicate to us the fruit of Christ's Paschal Mystery. We have access to the life of God through the sacred humanity of Jesus Christ. This is God's way.

The sacraments are also the work of Christ in that he is their author: he "instituted" them and handed them over to the Church, which is itself the sacrament of his continuing presence in the world, his mystical body. To return to an earlier theme, we know of no other way apart from the Church in which Christ himself has willed to be continually present and communicate himself to his chosen people. This is Christ's way. The sacraments of Christ are always, therefore, sacraments of the Church. They make her to be what she is — the Body of Christ. They reveal, most perfectly in the Eucharist, God's desire for ultimate communion with every one who is "in Christ."

The Seven Sacraments

There are seven sacraments which we receive from Christ, and among them there is a certain logic or ordering. Baptism, Confirmation, and Eucharist are called sacraments of *initiation* since they inaugurate the life of Christ in us, strengthen it, and bring it to fulfillment in our experience of receiving Christ's body and blood. We become a liturgical and sacramental people through these sacraments.

Penance and Anointing of the Sick are sacraments of *healing* for in them the Paschal Mystery is the remedy for what ails us, whether that be the spiritual ailment of sin or the physical burden of sickness and disease.

Finally, Matrimony and Holy Orders are the sacraments *at the service of communion,* for these make possible the continuation of all life in this world, actual physical life through the begetting of children in marriage, and spiritual life, sacramental and ecclesial, in Holy Orders.

The Catechism explains that three of these seven — Baptism, Confirmation, and Orders — confer a sacramental "character" or "seal." This is an indelible configuration of the person to Christ and to the Church. It cannot be reversed or taken away. This character — this marking of the baptized, confirmed, or ordained person as Christ's special possession — imparts a new destiny on that person. He or she is now disposed to the life of grace and protected by God's strength and power in a new way. This is clearly expressed when one celebrates the liturgy of the Church, for there one's full identity as a sharer in Christ's own priestly identity is manifest.

The Efficacy of the Sacraments

In speaking of what God does in the sacraments, the Catechism does not neglect what is required of the man or woman who comes to the sacraments. What is required is *faith*. The sacraments presuppose faith on the part of the one who is seeking to be saved through them. Even here the role of the Church is significant, for "the faith of the Church precedes the faith of the believer." Acting in the name and power of Christ, the Church invites us to faith, confers on us the sacraments of faith, and nourishes and develops faith in its sacramental liturgy. This is well expressed in the ancient Latin axiom *lex orandi lex credendi*; literally, "the law of prayer is the law of faith," or "the Church believes as she prays."

The dignity which the liturgy thus enjoys as a constitutive part of the tradition of faith puts it outside the power of priest or congregation in any way to change, delete, or manipulate it. The Church herself receives the sacraments from Christ and must guard them carefully so as not to stray from his divine will and intention. In the sacraments, our ways must be transformed into his ways.

The sacraments can never be simple historical reminiscences of the life and death of Christ. They are not a kind of adult "story-time" in salvation history. In the sacraments Christ *does* something. In Baptism it is Christ who baptizes. When the Church pours water over the infant's head and says, "I baptize you . . ." it is Christ who conforms this child to himself in his passion, death, and resurrection. It is Christ who sends the Spirit to confer the sacramental "character" on the newly baptized.

Because the sacraments are the actions of Christ, we say that they are "efficacious." This means that they actually communicate the grace that they signify. For this reason the Catechism uses the language of "actions," "powers," "makes present," "transforms," and "confers" when speaking of the sacraments. Since it is Christ who acts in the sacraments, their saving effects do not depend on the integrity and holiness of the minister or priest. They effect what they signify because of Jesus Christ — the one who is at work within the words and actions of each sacramental rite.

While we know that the fruitfulness of the sacrament for the individual depends on his or her dispositions in faith; nonetheless, in the sacraments Christ *always* pours out the gift of his life through the Holy Spirit. In Scripture, Christ reveals that the sacraments are necessary for our salvation (see Jn 3:5, Mt 28:19, Jn 6:53-54). His desire and design is that in the sacraments of his Church we would always have the means for deeper communion with him and through him a fuller share in the trinitarian life of love and communion.

The Climax of the Paschal Mystery in the Sacraments

The Catechism tells us that in the sacraments Christ not only communicates a share in his life now, but is preparing us for a final destiny of participating in his glory in eternity. The sacraments anticipate what we will be when the veil of our mortality has fallen away. The sacraments not only provide food and strength for the journey while we are on earth, but they give us a foretaste of heaven. In this way the sacraments are our guarantee of the new destiny that is ours, our future glory.

The liturgy of the Church is sacramental in nature because it makes present through signs and symbols the reality of the Paschal Mystery. Just as Christ is the "sacrament" of our relationship with God, so too the liturgy is the "sacrament" of Christ's continuing activity in the Church.

The central and climactic moments of this liturgical and sacramental activity are the seven sacraments instituted by Christ. The sacramental liturgy of the Church is the source of the sanctification of man and the gift of glory and praise to God. In Christ, God's thoughts and ways and man's thoughts and ways meet and become one. God becomes man that man might become God. Our transformation in Christ will bring us to ultimate communion with God.

Chapter 10

Sacraments of Initiation: Baptism, Confirmation, Eucharist

CATECHISM OF THE CATHOLIC CHURCH ¶1212 - ¶1419

Life is our most precious gift, thus we sometimes speak of the "miracle" of conception, birth, and development. Drawing upon the thought of Pope Paul VI, the Catechism discerns a certain parallel between the development of natural life and the development of our spiritual life. As a child is born, develops, and is nourished, so the Christian is born anew in Baptism, is strengthened in the sacrament of Confirmation, and is nourished in the food of eternal life, the Eucharist. These three are called the sacraments of Christian initiation since they lay the foundation for all Christian life and mark the beginning of the progressive development of that life in holiness and generous service to our neighbor.

The Catechism presents the sacraments of initiation as one continuous action of the Holy Spirit within each Christian person. They create new relationships to God: Baptism joins us to Christ in his Paschal Mystery; Confirmation imparts the special strength of the Holy Spirit; and the Eucharist, which completes the initiation process, unites us to Christ in his offering of himself as a perfect sacrifice to the Father. The sacraments of initiation are the actualization of growth into the ways of God and the Christian's gradual introduction into his life of knowledge and love. Taking each in turn, the Catechism considers the role of each sacrament of initiation in the history of salvation, provides a commentary on the liturgical rite of the sacrament, describes those being "initiated" into Christian life, and finally reviews the effects — the grace — of each sacrament.

Baptism

In commenting on the liturgy of Baptism, the Catechism roots its reflection on Christian initiation in the actual celebration of the Church's sacramental liturgy. Anyone who has participated in a Baptism can imbibe a theological understanding of the sacrament *through* the rite itself. *Lex orandi, lex credendi*: as the Church prays, she believes.

The very term "Baptism," which means literally to "plunge" or "immerse," captures the fundamental meaning of the sacrament. In the rite one is plunged into Christ's death and rises up from the water "a new creature." Catholics rarely witness a Baptism by "immersion" where the catechumen goes down into a pool and is three times immersed under the water and three times raised up. Usually we see the alternative form of pouring water on the head of the infant or catechumen. As a symbol of ritual death and of being raised to life, immersion replicates Christ's own death and resurrection. Regardless of the form used, it should not be forgotten that the newly baptized share in this mystery.

The Catechism employs the ancient words of St. Ambrose to illustrate that the source of this Baptism is the sacred humanity of Christ: "See where you are baptized, see where Baptism comes from, if not from the cross of Christ. There is the whole mystery: he died for you. In him you are redeemed, in him you are saved" (1225). This is the gift which Christ has given to his Church and which the apostles and their successors make available to all who believe and accept the Word of God.

The Catechism carefully outlines the dramatic transformation effected in the baptized by the Holy Spirit through the "water bath" and the trinitarian formula. We go down into the waters of Baptism to be purified from all sin, original sin and personal sins. We come forth from the waters of the font regenerated, a child of God through our new relationship with the only begotten Son. We receive sanctifying grace, a share in God's own life, which justifies us and bestows on us those benefits which will provide the means for living out the consequences of Baptism: the theological virtues which enable us to believe, hope in, and love God; the gifts of the Holy Spirit which provide the power to live and act according to the movements of the Spirit; and the moral virtues which allow us to grow in goodness. The whole organism of Christian supernatural life is rooted in Baptism.

Finally, we are made members of the Church of Christ in Baptism. The mystical Body of Christ is born at the baptismal font. We become members, one of another. Through Christ, we receive a share in the communion of life and love of the Father, Son, and Holy Spirit. This trinitarian communion is the foundation for a new relationship with all the other brothers and sisters of Christ. We no longer belong to ourselves, but to Christ who died and rose for us, and thus to the new People of God.

This irreversible membership in the Church reveals our share in her apostolic mission. Like Christ himself, we have been called not to be served, but to serve. The baptized are sharers in Christ's priestly work of giving glory to God and searching out our brothers and sisters who are in need.

This radical transformation of those who are baptized "into Christ," is expressed in the indelible spiritual "mark" or "character" on the one so reborn through water and the power of the Holy Spirit. The imprint of Christ's death and resurrection will forever "mark" the baptized; no sin can erase this "seal" of the Spirit which the baptized person carries into eternity. For this reason, Baptism is a once-and-for-all reality; it cannot be repeated.

The Catechism is clear in maintaining the present norm of the Baptism of infants, who are baptized, not in virtue of their own faith, but in light of the faith of their parents and that of the whole Church. Baptism is the sacrament of faith, but it is only within the faith of the Church that any individual can believe. Because even infants are born with a fallen human nature "tainted by original sin," they require Baptism in order to be freed from the power of darkness and to share in the freedom of the children of God. Parents and the Church are called to be nurturers of both physical and spiritual life. They must always do what is best for the child. In the case of Baptism, they must never deny the newly born the priceless grace of becoming a child of God.

Whether adult or infant, the sacrament requires faith, and that single requirement is already the gift of the Spirit. The faith required of one desiring Baptism is always less than perfect. It is a beginning. The Catechism is strong in its conviction that the "partnership" between the Holy Spirit and the Church is the necessary context for the celebration of the sacraments of Christ and their fruitful effect in the minds and hearts of believers. "When the Spirit encounters in us the response of faith which he has aroused in us, he brings about genuine cooperation. Through it the liturgy becomes the common work of the Holy Spirit and the Church" (1091).

In Baptism the Holy Spirit prepares us for the reception of Christ and makes present the mystery of Christ in the sacraments of initiation. We name the Holy Spirit as "teacher of the faith" for not only does he make present the Paschal Mystery of Christ, but he disposes the human person to receive the grace of each sacrament. The Holy Spirit and the Church cooperate to prepare the assembly by awakening faith in the hearts of believers and moving those hearts to conversion toward the heart of God and his will.

Confirmation

After Baptism, the next sacramental "moment" of initiation is that of Confirmation. In this sacrament the baptized are more perfectly bound to the Church. They are enriched with a special strength of the Holy Spirit which ratifies the commitment of each Christian to witness to the faith of Christ and to share in the work of evangelization by word and deed. Confirmation requires only that the person be already baptized and be in the state of grace, i.e., free from mortal sin.

Each Holy Thursday at the Chrism Mass the bishop consecrates the sacred oil of chrism for his diocese. Chrism is that special mixture of olive oil, spices, and perfume over which the bishop invokes the Father to send the Holy Spirit so that that chrism will become sacrament of that same Spirit. In the sacrament of Confirmation, the bishop anoints the forehead of the one receiving the sacrament, accompanied by the laying on of the hand and the words, "Be sealed with the Gift of the Holy Spirit."

In Confirmation our baptismal relationship with Christ is intensified and our new identity as sons and daughters of our heavenly Father is deepened and brought to a new level of maturity. Our bond with the Church is made more perfect. The gifts of the Holy Spirit received in Baptism are increased within us. Most significantly, we are given a special strength of the Spirit "to spread and defend the faith . . . as true witnesses of Christ, to confess the name of Christ boldly, and never to be ashamed of the Cross" (1303; cf. Council of Florence [1439]; DS 1319; LG, 11,12).

Like Baptism, Confirmation can be received only once; it too imprints on the soul an indelible spiritual mark — the "character" of Confirmation which is the "seal" of the Holy Spirit, the sign that Christ has clothed the Christian with "power from on high so that he may be his witness" (1304; cf. Council of Trent [1547]; DS 1609; Lk 24:48-49).

The Catechism urges that preparation for Confirmation should focus on the Christian's movement towards a more intimate union with Christ and greater familiarity with the Holy Spirit in order to be able to assume "the apostolic responsibilities of Christian life."

Eucharist

Communion with God always leads one to share in God's mission, the mission of Christ; that mission always returns to its source and goal — the communion of the Trinity. This is the dramatic transformation which the initiatory sacraments of Baptism and Confirmation "work" in us and prepare us for the culmination of Christian initiation, the sacrament of the Eucharist.

Contemporary Americans scour supermarket aisles looking for natural healthy foods, fat-free snacks, and new products to add zest to their seemingly boring diets. Paradoxically, in the face of this preoccupation with physical health and appearance, we learn from surveys and social analysts that fewer and fewer families actually sit down together for a meal on a regular basis. While we perhaps *eat* more than we should, we are losing the ability to *dine* together.

The Eucharist, God's bread for eternal life, can never be understood or appreciated without recovering the importance of meals shared as a fundamental expression of our human identity and destiny. The Eucharist cannot be reduced to an experience of "sharing," a profound concept now trivialized in much of the pseudo-spiritual literature of our time. Rather, in every meal, one reality, the mutual partaking of food, evokes another reality, a bonding, a unity, a communion of persons. As any parent or host knows, for a meal to be truly "successful" there must be some sacrifices: one must prepare what the guest or the family likes; the cook delights in providing what will taste good to the one who is, ideally, both friend and guest, and one's own preferences must often be set aside.

More to the point, food itself must be sacrificed. Food must disappear. It is consumed so that those present can come together in the communion of eating and in the communion of minds and spirits which common meals engender. The loss of a sense of meal-communion and meal-sacrifice is surely symptomatic of the loss of family cohesion in our society. Food and meals are about communion and sacrifice.

The Catechism's exposition of the Eucharist, the "sacrament of sacraments," is centered on these two aspects of meal and sacrifice. The Eucharist is "the source and summit of the Christian life" because it contains Christ in a most remarkable way, the whole mystery of Christ in an enduring, sacramental presence. Where there is Christ, there is the Church, and so the Eucharist is the source and summit of all ecclesial life and activity. We Christians are one because we are all joined to Christ. Our communion with him in the Eucharist begets our communion with one another and ultimately our communion with the blessed Trinity. Church unity and trinitarian communion flow from the side of Christ in the sacrament of the Eucharist.

The Catechism declares that the Eucharist is "the sum and summary of our faith" (1327) and for this reason it is always seen as the completion of the process of Christian initiation. Our relationship with Jesus Christ, established in Baptism and strengthened in Confirmation, is now brought to its fullest expression, our share in his own self-oblation in the Eucharist. At one and the same time, Christ gives himself to us and offers himself to the Father. In the Eucharist we are both the object of Christ's love for us and with him we become lovers of the Father.

Significantly, it was at a meal that Christ instituted the sacrament of the Eucharist. The Last Supper was the first Mass.

The use of bread and wine at sacred meals had a long history in Judaism. It symbolized the goodness of creation, for in bread and wine, natural products were transformed into food. Table fellowship, solemnized by the use of bread and wine, communicated a relationship of intimacy and mutual knowledge. To share a man's table was to be invited into the inner circle of the family; only trusted friends break bread together and share the cup of wine. In choosing the setting of the Passover meal, Jesus gave this ancient observance its definitive meaning and purpose — to be a memorial of his one perfect sacrifice on the cross, his Paschal Mystery, which would deliver all men from sin and death.

Christ's table fellowship with the apostles established a relationship of intimacy with himself; in turn it became a symbol of the deepest intimacy between himself and his Father. All fellowship must find its source in the communion of the Trinity. This table fellowship also anticipated what would happen after the Supper — Christ's passion, death, and resurrection. At the Last Supper the Paschal Mystery was made present in the sacrament of the Eucharist before it actually took place in time and history. The Mass stands outside of time and must be forever the sacrificial meal of the New Covenant; it is always a banquet and a sacrifice.

The Church obeys the command of Christ, "Do this is memory of me," by continuing to celebrate the Eucharist in every age and in every place where she exists. As the Catechism makes clear, the fundamental structure of the Mass has remained unchanged through the centuries. Beginning with the second century text of St. Justin Martyr, the Catechism offers a brief commentary on this unchanging structure. The teaching of the Catechism looks to the liturgy itself for the foundations of faith and doctrine. *Lex orandi, lex credendi:* as she prays, so does the Church believe.

The heart of the Catechism's theological consideration of the Eucharist as sacrifice and meal is trinitarian. The Eucharist is seen as the *thanksgiving* and *praise* to the Father; the sacrificial *memorial* of Christ and his body; and the *presence* of Christ by the power of his word and of his Spirit.

Eucharist literally means "thanksgiving." Christian Eucharist is the offering, the sacrifice, of *thanks* to God the Father for all that he has done for us from his first act of creation to the culminating gift of his love in the great gift of Jesus Christ, his Son, sent into the world because the Father "so loved the world." In the Eucharist the Church gives thanks in her own name and in the name of all creation. She *praises* the glory of God made so clearly manifest in the world, but knows that she can only do this through Christ — as we say in each Mass, "through him, with him, in him."

The Eucharist is a *memorial* of the sacrifice of the cross. It not only recalls what Christ has accomplished in his Paschal Mystery, but it makes that mystery present and applies it to the lives of those who share in the Eucharistic table. Just as Christ was able to make the Paschal Mystery present at the Last Supper before it actually occurred in time, so too the Church, through the power of the Holy Spirit, can make present this once-for-all sacrifice of Christ's life on the cross even after it has *happened.* The past is made present in the Eucharistic memorial. Christ expressed the sacrificial character of his death when he spoke of his body "given for you" and his blood "poured out for you." In the Mass, the Paschal Mystery of Christ, his perfect sacrifice, is forever present in the Church.

The Catechism is strong in its affirmation of the doctrine of the "real presence" of Christ in the Eucharist. As the Church prays the Eucharistic prayer, the action of the Holy Spirit brings about the conversion of bread and wine into Christ's body and blood. Christ becomes *present* in this sacrament.

Christ is present among us in many ways: in his Word, in the assembly of believers, in the priest, in the sacraments. All these are all "real" presences. The Eucharistic presence of Christ, however, is unique, for here the "*whole Christ is truly, really, and substantially* contained" (1374; Council of Trent [1551]; DS 1651). What was bread is no longer bread. What was wine is no longer wine. Though appearances remain the same in sight, smell, and taste, bread is now the body of Christ, God's bread, and wine is now the blood of Christ, God's wine. We name this the "real" presence because it is presence in the fullest sense.

It is that presence by which Christ, God and man, "makes himself wholly and entirely present" (1374; Paul VI, *Mysterium fidei*, 39). The Catechism borrows the words of St. Thomas Aquinas in explaining that this sacrament which, through the power of the Holy Spirit, contains Christ, enjoys the first place among all the sacraments as "the perfection of the spiritual life and the end to which all the sacraments tend" (1374; Aquinas, STh III, 73, 3c).

It is his immense love for us which prompted Christ to provide for his continuing presence among us in this way. This permanent memorial of his sacrifice is made present in a sacramental meal. Through Baptism we begin to share in the blessed Trinity's communion of life and love, a communion that will be consummated in the life of eternity. It is not surprising that Jesus, God and man, the very best of friends, should provide for us in this way. Friends, after all, want to be together. In the Eucharist, he is ever present, ever sacrificing himself for us, and ever the perfect host, providing all that we could desire or need — himself.

This sacrificial meal, celebrated on the table of the altar of Christ, is a call to deeper intimacy and communion than is possible in any other table fellowship, past, present, or future.

Like all important events, this meal calls for preparation. Mortal sin alone can keep us from the partaking of the Eucharistic banquet. Faith is the required preparation, and the humility to speak for ourselves the words of the centurion cited by the Catechism and repeated in every Mass, "Lord, I am not worthy that you should enter under my roof, but only say the word and my soul will be healed."

True spiritual hunger should bring us to the table of Christ's body and blood as often as possible — surely every Sunday, perhaps every day. Frequent Eucharistic communion feeds intimacy. The intimacy of friendship with Christ is the sure way to ultimate communion with God, Father, Son, and Holy Spirit. If there is grave sin in our lives, we must prepare for Holy Communion by going to the sacrament of Penance. Christ sets the table of forgiveness in order to feed us at the sacred banquet of his body and blood.

In outlining the fruits of Holy Communion, the Catechism insists that everything depends upon the truth that the Eucharist is a true communion with Christ. What food produces in our bodily life, the Eucharist accomplishes in our spiritual life. In Holy Communion the Holy Spirit "preserves, increases and renews the life of grace received in Baptism." When my body and blood encounters the body and blood of Christ in Holy Communion something happens. In this meeting, this communion, my relationship with Christ grows, develops, increases. As a consequence I am freed from venial sin and preserved from future mortal sin. Where there is Christ there cannot be sin. Holy Communion weans me from my attachment to sin and intensifies my attachment to the things of God, indeed my attachment to God himself. The Eucharist plunges me more deeply into the life of Christ, head and members. I am more deeply committed to the Church. And those whom Christ loved and preferred, the poor, become the object of my special love and generous concern. In this communion I become one with all those who are in Christ.

St. Augustine proclaims, "O sacrament of devotion! O sign of unity! O bond of charity!" This is the sacrament which prepares us for ultimate communion with God, the eternal banquet of glory and adoration and thanksgiving so beautifully described in the Book of Revelation.

"O sacred banquet in which Christ is received as food, the memory of his Passion is renewed, the soul is filled with grace and a pledge of the life to come is given to us."

Chapter 11

Sacraments of Healing: Penance and Anointing

CATECHISM OF THE CATHOLIC CHURCH ¶1420 - ¶1532

Today we put great stock in the healing professions. Medical doctors and a wide range of therapists are the new "priests" of our society. Hospitals and clinics serve as the new "temples" in which many modern people seek the strength and healing formerly sought only in religion. The cult of the individual and the individual's body is a new form of worship which involves rituals of self-help and exercise, both mental and physical, which promise a harvest of wholeness and contentment formerly ascribed only to the power of God. The sacraments of Penance and Anointing are just that — God's ways of providing the healing, the wholeness, and the peace and joy which can only be found through a renewed and authentic relationship with Jesus Christ.

Penance

In the Catechism, the sacraments of healing flow directly from the sacraments of Christian initiation. The new life in Christ which comes to us through Baptism can be weakened or even lost by sin. Just as that new life was strengthened in Confirmation, and nourished in the Eucharist, Christ continues his work of healing and restoring in the sacrament of Penance.

In his decision to institute the sacrament of Penance, Christ clearly illustrates his intention to be less a task master and more the dispenser of God's mercy, forgiveness, and love. He is not content merely to incorporate each Christian into his own life, though that in itself is a reality beyond our fondest hopes or imagination. As Good Shepherd and Divine Physician, he provides for every eventuality, most especially for our failure to be faithful to this gift of life and intimacy with the triune God.

Knowing the weakness of humanity, Christ knew Christian life to be an ongoing process of conversion. The wonder of the sacrament of Penance lies in Christ's provision not only of the means for our transformation into holiness, but his provision of the remedy to our hardness of heart, our sin, and our need to be won back to him again and again. Jesus faced the reality of sin which is an offense against God and disrupts the communion of faith and peace in his body, the Church. Where there is Christ, there is the Church. Every offense against God has consequences for the Church. Where one member of the body rises or falls, the fabric of the whole is affected. Sin is at once deeply personal and deeply ecclesial.

What Baptism, Confirmation, and Eucharist accomplish sacramentally within each of us must be lived out in the context of a frail human nature, weakened by original sin. In physical life a healing may be complete, but a certain weakness of joint or bone often perdures long after the illness or surgery. There is a parallel in the spiritual life. Sin is completely taken away in Baptism, but there are the "traces" of sin within us, a certain inclination to the weakness of egoism, the pride of preferring our ways to those of God and the consequent rebellion against his will. The Catholic tradition names this lack of facility in choosing the good, which remains even after Baptism, as "concupiscence." The Catechism warns that the "struggle of conversion" is a central reality in realizing the fullness of what is begun in the sacraments of initiation.

We know that conversion is one of the principal themes of the preaching of Jesus. Christ's call to turn from evil and believe the Gospel is made a reality within us at Baptism. This is what the Catechism calls "the first and fundamental conversion" (1427). There is yet the "second conversion" which continues throughout the whole lifetime of the Christian: the "movement of the 'contrite heart,' drawn and moved by grace to respond to the merciful love of God who loved us first" (1428; Ps 51:17; cf. Jn 6:44; 12:32; I Jn 4:10).

Conversion continues as long as we live, but is before all else the work of grace. It is God who gives the strength to begin anew. The radical change which God works in us through the grace of Jesus Christ does not aim first of all at outward works of discipline and penance, but at the depths of the human heart and personality. It is a deeply interior conversion which seeks expression in "visible signs, gestures and works of penance." Penance is God's sacramental plan for celebrating the triumph of Christ over sin and our progressive conversion into Christ. This ongoing transformation which prepares us for the ultimate happiness of trinitarian communion is a reality not only for the individual but for the whole community of the Church.

The Catechism stresses the continuity in the fundamental structure of the sacrament despite many changes in its external liturgical expression. There are two equally essential elements: what *we* must do under the influence of the Holy Spirit: contrition, confession, and satisfaction; what *God* does through the intervention of the Church in giving "absolution."

Contrition is "sorrow of the soul and detestation for the sin committed, together with the resolution not to sin again" (1451; Council of Trent [1551]: DS 1676). This quality of the inner self is of primary importance and becomes the motive for disclosing one's sins to the priest. All mortal sins must be confessed in kind and number. In this way one who is burdened with serious sin must face the truth of his disorder and take responsibility for personal sin. Such "tearing open" of the hidden weaknesses and sins of the human heart is considered therapeutic in many religions, but in this sacrament we expose the hidden recesses of our minds and hearts to Christ the Shepherd, whose cross robbed sin of its power to enslave us.

It is Christ to whom we confess our sins in the sacrament of Penance and Christ alone, through the blood of his cross, who forgives our sins through the priest, his instrument. As successors to the apostles, bishops and priests continue this ministry which Christ entrusted to them when he declared that what they bind or loose on earth will be bound or loosed in heaven. While "absolution takes away sin . . . it does not remedy all the disorders sin has caused" (1459; cf. Council of Trent [1551]: DS 1712). Spiritual health requires more: that we make amends for our sins, that we make "satisfaction" by works of prayer, charity, or some act of Christian asceticism. We normally speak of doing the "penance" which the priest assigns during the time of "going to confession."

The expansion of the title of the sacrament to "Penance and Reconciliation" is precisely to express its full meaning. Not only are our sins forgiven and taken away, but we are reconciled again with God and with his Church. Reconciliation with God is the purpose of the sacrament. Since the Church is God's continuing presence in the world, our ecclesial communion, marred by sin, is restored and strengthened.

In his sacramental work of reconciliation Christ also strengthens us for future encounters with evil, the struggle with our own concupiscence and any temptation which may come our way. The sacrament of Penance and Reconciliation is the "sacrament of the present" by taking away our sins and reconciling us to God and his Church. But it is the "sacrament of the future" by protecting us from the influence of evil and strengthening us in our "second conversion." It anticipates the judgment of God which faces each of us at the end of life.

The sacrament of Penance and Reconciliation, like all sacraments, finds its fulfillment in leading us to Christ in the Eucharist. All sin weakens us spiritually, but mortal sin excludes us from participation in the Eucharist — that communion which most perfectly reflects the beatitude of heaven. Penance and Reconciliation restores us to a right relationship with God and opens the way for Holy Communion, wherein Christ's own body and blood become our nourishment for life eternal. Penance, or "Confession" as we sometimes call it, leads us to the altar and is, in the final analysis, about the Eucharist, and the Eucharist is about Christ's own communion of trinitarian life. God's delicacy and gentleness in the sacrament of Penance and Reconciliation lead us to his own glory revealed in Christ. When we need healing, Christ is among us in the sacraments, healing us and making us whole. His deepest desire is to lead us to ultimate communion.

Anointing of the Sick

The realities of illness and suffering cannot be avoided in human life. In illness, the Catechism remarks, man "experiences his powerlessness, his limitations, and his finitude" (1500). The danger of discouragement and despair in the midst of physical affliction and misery can only be overcome by the reality of faith and the attempt to find meaning in the mystery of God's providence. In his endurance of pain and suffering, Christ reveals the redemptive significance of all human suffering. In the mystery of the cross "he makes their miseries his own" (1505). Christ's "preferential love for the sick" (1503) has drawn Christians of every age to follow his example in caring for those who suffer in body and soul. In the Gospels it is the same Christ who so often urged the sick to believe. Human sickness and suffering can become salvific when accepted and understood in faith.

The sacraments are the very way in which Christ continues to "touch" us in order to heal us. This is particularly true of the sacrament of Anointing of the Sick. While each Christian may be called to carry the cross of any sickness or suffering which they endure, nonetheless Christ directs the Church to "heal the sick." The sacrament of Anointing is that special sacrament intended to strengthen those "who are being tried by illness" (1511).

As soon as there is any danger of death from sickness, the priest is called to pray over the sick, to lay hands on them, and to anoint them. This sacramental action on the part of the Church effects a new gift of the Holy Spirit in the sick person: the gifts of strength and courage to face the difficulties of suffering and pain. This grace of the Holy Spirit is meant to lead the sick person "to healing of the soul, but also of the body if such is God's will" (1520; cf. Council of Florence [1439]: DS 1325), and "if he has committed sins, he will be forgiven" (1520; Jas 5:15; cf. Council of Trent [1551]: DS 1717).

The Catechism recognizes that God gives to some a "special charism of healing" as a manifestation of the grace of the risen Christ. The prayers of these "healers" do not always obtain a cure of sickness so ardently desired. In the sacrament of Anointing it is the promised spiritual healing which is always given — the spiritual healing of the soul, even the forgiveness of sin, and the support of the prayer of the Church. In Anointing one is joined to the passion of Christ, his own experience of pain and suffering, and one is prepared for the final journey. Just as Penance prepares us for future judgment, Anointing fortifies us at the end of our earthly life as we face the final struggles "before entering the Father's house" (1523; Council of Trent [1551]: DS 1694).

For a long period of time Anointing was called "Extreme Unction" and was closely linked with the moment of impending death. The Church insists that Anointing should be given "as soon as anyone of the faithful begins to be in danger of death from sickness or old age" (1514; SC 73; cf. CIC, cann. 1004, 1; 1005; 1007; CCEO, can. 738). The Catechism echoes the teaching of Vatican II in explaining that the final sacrament for the Christian is not Anointing, but Viaticum, that is, Eucharist, received at the moment of "passing over" to the Father. This sacrament of Christ "once dead and now risen" is the final sacrament of passing over from this world to the life of trinitarian communion and love.

Chapter 12

Sacraments at the Service of Communion: Orders and Matrimony

CATECHISM OF THE CATHOLIC CHURCH ¶1533 - ¶1666

In the Old Covenant God chose a people from among the nations to be peculiarly his own. It was precisely in belonging to this community of faith in the one true God that a relationship with God and a hope for salvation could be realized within the individual. This "belonging" was the birthright of each Jew.

The coming of Jesus Christ in the New Covenant radically changed that situation. Now it is through one's personal relationship with Jesus that a person becomes a member of God's household, whether Jew or Greek, male or female, slave or freeman. All have access to intimacy with God through faith in Jesus Christ, and one is thereby a member of his body — the Church. The sacraments of the New Dispensation initiate, nurture, and develop this personal relationship with God and our participation in the holiness and justice of his new Israel, the Church of Jesus Christ.

The sacraments of Christian initiation — Baptism, Confirmation, and Eucharist — establish this relationship of friendship within us and continue the process of growth and maturity in the life of faith. The sacraments of healing — Penance and Anointing of the Sick — serve as remedies when obstacles to our faith such as sin and sickness occur in our lives. In all five of these sacraments the individual is the object, the recipient, of an increasingly greater share in the Paschal Mystery of Christ. Consequently, one is more deeply related to and attached to the priestly community of the Church.

In the "sacraments at the service of communion" a new direction can be discerned. In Holy Orders and Matrimony, the individual receives a new outpouring of the Holy Spirit in order to be at the disposal of the spiritual good of the Church. If we can describe the other sacraments as primarily for the benefit of the individual, these two must be described as placing the individual at the service of others. They are consecrated for the good of those who are their brothers and sisters in the flesh and in the faith.

This principle of self-transcendence, an expression of Christ's own self-oblation, is at the heart of the Catechism's account of the sacraments of Holy Orders and Matrimony. The Christian person who is ordained or married no longer lives for himself, but for the good of the community. In Marriage it is the family, the good of the spouse and of the children, which is the object of one's concerns, love, and dedication. In Holy Orders one's entire life must be centered on the good of the faithful and on the spiritual needs of God's Church. In each case one's life is no longer one's own.

Holy Orders

The Catechism's exposition of the sacrament of Holy Orders is strongly Eucharistic. Just as the redemptive sacrifice of Christ is made present in the Eucharist, his priesthood is made present through the "ministerial" priesthood. There is only one priest and one priesthood, that of Jesus Christ. His unique sacrifice, his Paschal Mystery, established Christ as the one true priest of the New Covenant. Jesus, while still on earth, entrusted to his apostles his mission and his priesthood and sent them into the whole world to continue his priestly work long after his ascension and glorification. This is the sacrament of Holy Orders. "Only Christ is the true priest, the others being only his ministers" (1545; St. Thomas Aquinas, *Hebr*. 8.4).

The Catechism uses the term "ministerial" to distinguish the two ways of participating in the one priesthood of Jesus Christ. In Baptism every Christian becomes a partaker in the one priesthood of Christ. This "baptismal" priesthood, common to all believers, is exercised by each Christian according to his particular vocation by taking part in the sacramental liturgy of the Church, carrying out the duties of his state in life, praying, and performing works of charity. The "ministerial or hierarchical" priesthood is at the service of the common priesthood of the baptized. While those ordained to Holy Orders share in the baptismal priesthood, the sacrament of Orders confers on them an essentially different configuration to the one Priest — Jesus Christ.

The ministerial priesthood is a *means* by which Christ continues to help the faithful in the unfolding of the baptismal grace of their common priesthood. Like Baptism and Confirmation, Holy Orders imprints the ordained with an indelible spiritual mark. One is a priest in time and in eternity. Through the laying on of hands and the prayer of consecration, the Holy Spirit conforms the ordained to Christ as Priest, Teacher, and Pastor. As Baptism and Confirmation find their fulfillment in the Eucharist, so does Holy Orders find its perfect expression in the Eucharistic action of the priest. He is most himself, most truly a priest of Christ, when he stands at the altar and feeds God's people with God's life-giving Word and the life-giving body and blood of Christ, God's only begotten Son. The Eucharist reveals to us the true nature and identity of the priest.

The Catechism uses the rich language of the tradition to explain that in the sacrament of Holy Orders, Christ is present to his Church as "Head of his Body, Shepherd of his flock, high priest of the redemptive sacrifice, Teacher of Truth" (1548). When we speak of the priest as acting *in persona Christi Capitis*, (cf. LG, 10, 28) we indicate the way in which Christ, as head of the Church, is made visible in the midst of the community of believers. In the same way the priest acts "in the name of the whole Church" (1552), in the name of the whole community of believers before God. Most particularly in the prayer and offering of the Eucharist, the priest must present to God the needs and desires of his people, just as Christ himself prayed to the Father in loud cries and tears with prayer and supplication. Just as Christ is the perfect communication of God to man, Christ the priest is the perfect communication of man to God. This communication of God to man and man to God is the beginning of that eternal communion of love which is our trinitarian destiny. The Christian priest is dedicated to this mutual exchange between God and man.

The Catechism affirms the long tradition of ordaining only males to the priesthood. No one has a right to receive the sacrament of Holy Orders. The Church recognizes herself to be bound by the decision of Christ himself. For this reason "the ordination of women is not possible" (1577).

There are three "degrees" of Holy Orders: bishop, priest, and deacon. The bishop receives from the Spirit the grace to guide and defend the Church "with strength and prudence as father and pastor" (1586). The priest, co-worker with the bishop, is likewise conformed to Christ the priest in order to proclaim the Word of God and to celebrate the sacramental liturgy of the Church, especially the Eucharist. The deacon, in collaboration with the bishop and priest, is "strengthened by sacramental grace . . . dedicated to the People of God . . . in the service of the liturgy, of the Gospel, and of works of charity" (1588; LG, 29).

Matrimony

Turning to the sacrament of Matrimony, the Catechism underscores the dignity of this sacrament and the strong role that the grace of the Holy Spirit plays in making a life of shared love and fidelity a realistic possibility for Christian couples. God is the author of Marriage; it is his intention that Marriage should reflect the deepest identity of its author, divine love. God created man out of love and calls him to love. So declares the Catechism. Love is the "fundamental and innate vocation of every human being" (1604).

Marriage is intended to be an image, a true reflection, of that mutual love which is God's inner life, Father, Son, and Holy Spirit. The mutual love of spouses and the fruitfulness of their unity of life and love expressed in the conception, birth, and education of children becomes a sign of that community of love which is God himself. Marriage requires fidelity and permanence, what the tradition calls "indissolubility," because God is who he is, a Trinity of persons who live in perfect love, and has willed Marriage to be the fundamental human expression and communication of that love.

The fulfillment of so lofty a vocation requires the grace of God, the grace of Christ, especially in light of the disorder introduced into the world and the human heart by sin and concupiscence. Christ himself provides this necessary grace in establishing the reality of Marriage as a sacrament of his presence. Thus it is Jesus Christ who confirms the goodness of Marriage and promises that fidelity and indissolubility are now possible for the Christian couple who will follow him in his Paschal Mystery.

The grace of Christian Marriage "is a fruit of Christ's cross, the source of all Christian life" (1615). The Catechism names this, "Marriage in the Lord." The union of two in one flesh which symbolizes the union of Christ with his Church is another reminder of that Eucharistic communion which is a foretaste of the eternal communion that is the fulfillment of life in Christ. It is he alone, Jesus the Christ, who binds a man and woman together and brings their union to its perfection.

In the course of its consideration of Marriage, the Catechism treats of yet one more Christian vocation: virginity for the sake of the kingdom. "Both the sacrament of Matrimony and virginity for the sake of the Kingdom of God come from the Lord himself" (1620). Marriage "in the Lord" is a reality of the present age which must, as we know, pass away. Virginity, is a powerful sign of that bond with Christ which will never pass away.

Esteem for virginity and the recognition of the dignity of Marriage go hand in hand in Christian doctrine and thought; they are "inseparable and they reinforce each other" (1620). Christ calls us in a variety of ways, but all are destined for the same heavenly beatitude which is to share his life of love and communion.

Chapter 13

The Liturgy, the Sacraments, and the Life of Prayer

CATECHISM OF THE CATHOLIC CHURCH ¶2558 - ¶2682

The Catechism's account of God's search for man is, for many, too good to be true. The divine persistence in issuing repeated invitations to the intimacy of friendship and the divine provision of the means to realize this relationship of love seem to make things too easy for man.

This uneasiness with the generosity of God is only intensified when confronted with the mystery of the Incarnation and the mystery of the Church and its sacramental liturgy, the celebration of the Paschal Mystery of Jesus Christ. Here, the Catechism insists, God continues to take the initiative. The Holy Spirit offers to each of us the first movements of faith, nurtures those beginnings and brings them to fulfillment in Baptism and the other sacraments. Our transformation into the likeness of Christ depends solely on God and the power of his grace to move us to accept his invitation to trinitarian communion.

Part Two of the Catechism is a systematic exploration of how God initiates, nourishes, and completes this life of divine and ecclesial relationship through the liturgy and the sacraments. The hesitation of Christian men and women to believe that such a gift and destiny cannot be earned or achieved, but is completely God's free gift freely given, requires that the Catechism sketch out in greater detail the effects of this divine initiative and persistence in the individual. Part Four of the Catechism, "Christian Prayer," outlines the response of the individual to life in Christ as offered and effected by the liturgy and the sacraments, a personal relationship with the living and true God. "This relationship is prayer."

Liturgy and Prayer

What the liturgy proclaims, celebrates, makes present, and communicates must be accepted and continued deep within the heart of the Christian person. "Prayer internalizes and assimilates the liturgy during and after its celebration" (2655). Prayer is one of the graces which the liturgy offers to those who come in faith to the ecclesial celebration of the Paschal Mystery. Contemporary spiritual writers speak of the "liturgy of the altar" and the "liturgy of the heart": liturgy and the response of prayer. What begins in the church sanctuary must continue in the innermost sanctuary of the believer's heart and abide long after a particular celebration has ended. The heart's capacity for prayer is itself the fruit of the sacrament of Baptism, where one is joined to Christ and made a sharer in his priesthood, the priesthood of the baptized. Each time we celebrate the liturgy, each time we pray, we exercise this baptismal priesthood, we become more like Christ, the one true Priest of the New Covenant.

Prayer is less something that we "do" and more the actualization of what has been given to us. Prayer, as everything else in the Christian life, is God's gift to us rather than our gift to God. Prayer is our God-given response to God's initiative of self-revelation and self-communication. It begins in the liturgy and the sacraments, but it must take root and grow in the depths of the human heart. "The heart is our hidden center, beyond the grasp of our reason and of others; only the Spirit of God can fathom the human heart and know it fully" (2563).

The Holy Spirit engenders and develops within the deepest recesses of each person a vital relationship of love and mutual communion with the triune God throughout one's whole lifetime. What is begun in Baptism and Confirmation is continued in the sacramental liturgy of the Church, most especially of the Eucharist, for Christian prayer is always communion with Christ and his Church. Christ, through the power of the Spirit, leads us to the Father where we can share the fullness of trinitarian love and communion. "Thus, the life of prayer is the habit of being in the presence of the thrice-holy God and in communion with him" (2565).

The School of Prayer

The Catechism portrays the liturgy as the fundamental "school of prayer." It is first of all in the liturgy that the human heart learns to murmur sentiments of adoration, petition, intercession, thanksgiving, and praise. The ancient axiom *lex orandi, lex credendi,* "the law of prayer is the law of belief," reminds us of this. The Church's sacramental liturgy is the rule and norm of all Christian prayer; authentic spiritual formation must begin there. As the work of Christ, the liturgy has the power to instruct and guide us into the deepest experiences of prayer. In it, the power of the Holy Spirit brings to each Christian the fruits of Christ's sacred humanity. For some Catholics "going to Mass" may be the fulfillment of a minimal requirement of their faith. In reality, it is the privileged moment when one encounters the Holy Spirit who prays in us, transforms us, and prepares us for our ultimate destiny in Christ, trinitarian communion. Formation in prayer flows from liturgical formation.

Within the community of the Christian family, children first learn of God and the things of God. From their earliest years they are taught the correct responses at Mass, appropriate behavior in Church, and the meaning of what is happening at the altar and in the hearts of believers. The emphasis of the Second Vatican Council on "full and active participation" is founded on this vital and efficacious link between worship and personal prayer. Holiness comes to us through Christ who gives himself to us, unites us to himself, in the liturgy and sacraments of the Church. The connection between the altar and the human heart is immediate and intimate. It must never be broken.

From Liturgy to Prayer

The Catechism explains that this movement from liturgy to prayer is not haphazard. In Baptism the Holy Spirit lays the foundation of the life of faith in the heart of the believer. Faith, hope, and charity — the theological virtues — are part of the Spirit's baptismal gift of new life. The whole life of prayer and Christian morality are dependent upon these foundational habits or dispositions imparted in Baptism. Whether we pray to the Father, the Son, or the Holy Spirit, we always pray *through* Christ, in whose death and resurrection we have died to sin and been raised to new life. We believe that the Lord can and will fulfill his promises to us. We have a certain hope that what he has begun he will bring to completion. Having known his love, it is possible for us to love him in return.

Within the context of this dynamic relationship between liturgy and prayer, between Part Two and Part Four, the Catechism considers the long tradition of saints, mystics, doctors, and theologians who have written about the nature and experience of Christian prayer. From this vast body of literature about prayer, the fruit of centuries of experience, certain basic characteristics emerge as typical of all prayer. Just as the sacramental liturgy of the Church is *the* norm for Christian prayer, the writings of the saints provide another normative guide for Christians sincerely seeking union with God.

There are as many ways of prayer and praying as there are Christians. Each person is led by the Spirit and "taught" the way of prayer and intimacy with God. The important distinctions between vocal prayer, meditation, and contemplative prayer offer a road map for those needing direction in the wondrous adventure of developing a spiritual life.

Vocal prayer, taught by Jesus himself in the Our Father, gives shape, gives words, to the movements of the heart. It is fundamental to the experience of Christian prayer.

Meditation is an activity of the mind, a silent prayer that seeks to discipline our fickle and wandering thoughts so that we can focus on the true meaning of the Christian life, accept its deepest consequences, and recognize the obstacles within ourselves to true communion with God.

In *contemplative prayer*, that most deeply interior movement of the heart, our attention is fixed on the Lord himself. "I look at him and he looks at me."

The way of prayer, founded upon and fed by the liturgy, is not an easy road. Because we are busy people, because we are weak and preoccupied with ourselves, it is difficult to set aside the time and to establish the quiet needed for the journey of prayer. The liturgy spills over into a life of prayer and recollection, but the obstacles and distractions are many. When we finally settle down to pray, thoughts of responsibilities, of needs, of sufferings, crowd in on our minds and hearts. Sometimes we are tempted to daydream or fantasize about the goods and pleasures of this world.

The perseverance required of one who would become a man or woman of prayer is considerable. It is only possible to one who depends completely on Christ. Only his grace, the grace of the Paschal Mystery, will suffice.

Each Christian must learn to trust the grace of Jesus Christ, communicated to us in the sacraments and nourishing within us the life of prayer, meditation, and contemplation. The tutelage of the Holy Spirit results in what the Catechism calls "humble vigilance of the heart." We are children of our heavenly Father, made so by our incorporation into the firstborn Son. We must learn the way of childlike confidence in God.

Mary, the mother of Jesus, is the great icon of Christian prayer. Her prayerful "yes" at the moment of the Annunciation led her to the cross of Calvary and finally to the glory of the Assumption. Praying to her and with her, we will be led into the heart of the Church, into the heart of Christ — into the very heart of God.

Chapter 14

Life in Christ: The Catechism's Moral Anthropology

CATECHISM OF THE CATHOLIC CHURCH ¶1701 - ¶1784

Many people regard leading the moral life as a daunting challenge, as if observing the norms of Christian conduct meant constant struggle. It may seem odd, then, that the Catechism describes the moral life in terms of the Holy Spirit, grace, the Gospel beatitudes, sin and forgiveness, the virtues, and the twofold commandment of love. Are these matters that evoke mere striving and effort, an ethos of pure duty and stark will power? Clearly not.

The Catechism offers an alternative answer: the moral life more as a craft than a duty. In the Church of Christ, the believer learns about moral truth and, through the power of the Holy Spirit, develops the capacity to mold good deeds with ease, promptness, and joy. Once this "craft" of good living is acquired in grace, the members of the Church lead the moral life as if by second nature.

The Human Person: Made in God's Image

As the only creature on earth that God has willed for himself, the human person enjoys a central place among God's creatures. With the angels, man alone can join the intelligent chorus of praise and worship that God welcomes from his entire creation. Since we are intelligent creatures, our human nature necessarily reaches its final perfection "in wisdom, which gently draws the human mind to look for and to love what is true and good. Filled with wisdom man is led through visible realities to those which cannot be seen" (GS, 15). In the Catechism, this view of man grounds the presentation of the moral life, which it describes as a life lived in Christ.

The universal testimony of the Scriptures and the earliest witnesses of the Christian tradition affirm that every human being embodies the image of God. This godly image establishes the dignity of the human person. The saints teach that the image of God in us resembles the image of a sovereign on a coin: what bears the image possesses an entirely different nature from what it images. At the same time, the image accounts for our movement toward God. Each human person experiences, in some way, an ordering toward God; moreover, the desire for God forms a constitutive part of human existence. Because sin frustrates this desire, only Christ "reveals man to himself and brings to light his most high calling" (GS, 22).

The image of God exists in humankind in three ways. First, we can speak about a natural image of God, of which freedom is "an outstanding manifestation" (1705). In the natural order, this image can achieve only an aptitudinal conformity with the living God. The God so attained in knowledge is reached not within the divine self-disclosure of supernatural revelation, not as a Trinity of Persons, but rather from afar as the Source of all Being. God then is desired and pursued only as the Highest Good and as the principle of all goodness in the world, as known and desired solely through the contemplation of the being and goodness of creation.

Secondly, that image of God that is only potentially and aptitudinally conformed to the divine Persons by nature — and which "images" defectively owing to the wounds of human sinfulness — actually becomes a perfected image of God through the conformity to God progressively wrought by grace. For only the grace of Christ makes us God's adopted children. The virtues and commandments illumine and instruct us in our obligations as God's graced sons and daughters in the only Son.

Since this grace perdures unto the glory of life everlasting, the created image of God reaches its final and fullest existential state when the soul beholds God face to face. About this third moment, St. Paul writes: "Now the one who has prepared us for this very thing is God, who has given us the Spirit as a first installment" (II Cor 5: 5). The third part of the Catechism explains how the believer, who carries the image of God, should live so as to move from grace to glory.

Human Flourishing and the Call to Beatitude

The call to beatific fellowship with God means that man possesses an openness to communion with God. Good moral theology must respect the ordering of the image of God to its God-given ends. "He who paints our soul in the likeness of the blessed One," writes Gregory of Nyssa, "describes in words all that produces beatitude; and he says first: Blessed are the poor in spirit, because theirs is the Kingdom of Heaven." To describe Christian moral theology as teleological (from the Greek *telos*: pertaining to ultimate ends) means nothing more than this.

Moral theories that deny that the dynamism of human perfection unfolds through freely achieved virtuous acts propose other models to guide and explain human behavior. Utilitarian consequentialism judges morality somewhat mathematically on the basis of a putatively calculable "overall good" accomplished for the largest number. Deontological (from the Greek *deon*: pertaining to duty) theories appeal to pure duty or the obligation to follow a rationally constructed moral norm. The Catechism develops a teleological or end-centered model that begins with a description of the state of Christian perfection to which all men are called. "Acting is morally good when the choices of freedom are in conformity with man's true good and thus express the voluntary ordering of the person towards his ultimate end: God himself, the supreme good in whom man finds his full and perfect happiness" (VS, 72).

Next, the Catechism considers what comprises happiness for all men and women, what makes for the good of the person. What is this happiness? St. Augustine's cry in the *Confessions* sums up the Christian response: "You have made us for yourself, O Lord, and our hearts are restless until they rest in thee." As a theological term, "beatitude" designates specifically Christian happiness — that is, the realization of our human desire to see God. Insofar as the scriptural beatitudes (Mt 5:3-12) promise aspects of the good that open the believer up to eternal life, they are at the heart of the Christian vocation.

The human person's joyful possession of the beatific vision constitutes the consummation of the moral life. For this reason, the Catechism begins by considering beatitude in itself: God as he is, the highest

Goodness. It is because we are made for loving God that we must also love what belongs to God. First of all, this means loving our neighbor. This love preserves and respects that dignity of the creation which is the primordial sign of the divine goodness.

While there is no natural counterpart to the life of Christian excellence, it is nonetheless possible to identify a natural form of flourishing in the human virtues. Human goods, especially contemplation of the truth, promote authentic happiness. To be sure, the Christian must pursue these in a distinctive way. But one does not require Christian faith to recognize and to a certain extent begin to practice the virtues requisite to integral human fulfillment.

"It is possible by means of human works to acquire moral virtues," writes St. Thomas Aquinas, "in so far as they produce good works that are directed to an end not surpassing the natural power of man: and when they are acquired thus, they can be without charity, even as they were in many of the Gentiles." However, he continues, "in so far as they produce good works in proportion to a supernatural last end, thus they have the character of virtue, truly and perfectly; and cannot be acquired by human acts, but are infused by God." Natural and infused virtues must be distinguished from each other because effects must be proportioned to the principles from which they flow, and the effect of a limited natural rectitude must be distinguished from the effect of that rectitude directing us to the supernatural vision of God. Since the human creature was from the beginning created in the state of sanctifying grace, one finds natural and infused virtue profoundly intertwined in the given historical order of fallen and redeemed nature. Yet natural and infused virtue are distinct.

St. Thomas Aquinas identifies fifty-some natural human virtues that constitute integral human fulfillment in the human person. Other descriptions are possible. But the fundamental insight, both into the natural human virtues considered in themselves and into these virtues as elevated by grace, is indispensable for Christian moral teaching. In the order established by supernatural grace, each one of these virtues finds its perfection in charity which, according to St. Paul, forms the permanent heart of beatitude. Thus the Catechism states: "The beatitude of eternal life is a gratuitous gift of God. It is supernatural, as is the grace that leads us there" (1727).

Happiness is the cleaving to God as the all-fulfilling object of human knowing and loving. The axiom "grace perfects nature" (*gratia perficit naturam*) represents a concise statement of how the Catechism conceives the way that human flourishing conduces or leads to Christian beatitude. This happiness made St. Gregory of Nyssa think of the dizziness of a man who looks down into the depths of the sea from the top of a mountain. "In the same way," he says, "my soul grows dizzy when it hears the great voice of the Lord saying: 'Blessed are the clean of heart, for they shall see God.'" Because only God can fulfill the expectations of the human heart, the Catechism encourages us to evaluate all human actions according to how completely they draw a person to union with the living God — how they make one "clean of heart." St. Augustine underscores the value of this approach: "Blessed the one who knows Thee, even were he to know nothing else."

Human Freedom

The Catechism teaches that the same divine plan which establishes the rightness of the moral order also constitutes human nature as a specific kind of being, one that enjoys the capacity to choose freely. Thus, as Pope John Paul II recently wrote, it is sound to say that "God's plan poses no threat to man's genuine freedom; on the contrary, the acceptance of God's plan is the only way to affirm that freedom" (VS, 45).

Freedom characterizes properly human acts. If autonomy consists in being "part-author" of our lives and activity (as we are subjects of nature, human community, and human history, as well as of divine providence, complete "self-authorship" is an impossibility), then surely the more comprehensive the good realized through our freedom the more perfected is this freedom. The immutable good of beatific vision and love, achieved through perseverance in graced acts of virtue, reveals a good whose profundity and permanence bestows sacral meaning upon human liberty: "the glorious liberty of the sons of God."

Divine guidance does not override free choice since, as Aquinas says, "the children of God are led by the Holy Spirit not as slaves, but as free people. . . . The Holy Spirit so inclines us to act as to make us act voluntarily, inasmuch as he makes us love, and not slavishly. . . . Since the Holy Spirit inclines the will, through love, toward the true good toward which the will is inclined by nature, he takes away both the slavery whereby the person having been made a slave of passion and sin, acts against the [natural tendency] of the will; and also the slavery whereby, contrary to the movement of his will, a person acts according to the law like a slave of the law, not a friend. That is why the apostle says in 2 Corinthians 3:17, 'Where the Spirit of the Lord is, there is freedom,' and in Galatians 5:18, 'If you are led by the Spirit, you are not under the law.' "

While sin does not annihilate human freedom, our own sins and the effects of original sin in the world make it difficult always to choose the good. The Pauline epistles repeatedly affirm that Christ made each of his members free so that they could find their perfection in him. "For you were called for freedom, brothers. But do not use this freedom as an opportunity for the flesh; rather, serve one another through love. . . . Now those who belong to Christ [Jesus] have crucified the flesh with its passions and desires" (Gal 5:13, 24). The Christian paradox is that the person who dies with Christ rises with him to new life and freedom.

In sum: complete human happiness lies only in the happiness which God authors and which we freely embrace. But this does not mean that beatitude is only for the few. When Christ himself promises the Good Thief, "Today you will be with me in Paradise" (Lk 23:43), the Gospel assures us that paradise remains open even to the most miserable among men and women.

Chapter 15

Actions, Emotions, and Conscience

CATECHISM OF THE CATHOLIC CHURCH ¶1749 - ¶1802

Pope John Paul II continues to remind the Church and the world that a happy society is one in which moral conscience informs each member of the group. The Second Vatican Council declares conscience to be "a sanctuary. There he is alone with God whose voice echoes in his depths" (GS, 16). Today, some people appeal to conscience in order to excuse the failure to observe moral truth. But when they set themselves up as their own moral authority, they not only stifle the voice of conscience, they also frustrate their desire for happiness. As the poet reminds us, God hounds the human creature so that he or she cannot easily run away.

Morality and Right Reason

"Man is made to God's image, and this implies that he is intelligent and free to judge and master himself." The roots of morality lie in freedom. But human freedom requires direction. This guidance comes from the virtue of prudence, which shapes each human action so that everything we do achieves an end which respects human nature itself, and thus perfects the human person who acts. Whereas the other moral virtues of justice, fortitude, and temperance each shape one of our appetitive capacities (the will and emotions), prudence directs the moral conscience itself. This first of the cardinal virtues puts reason into emotion, so as to ensure that moral truth always informs moral choice.

Why is sound reason so important for making a good moral choice? In the first place, reason means human intelligence. But is this reason independent? Plainly not, since it in turn is measured by the reason in things, as when one asks, "What is the reason for the sun's coming up in the morning?" In response one names some real cause, something in the nature of things, e.g., "The rotation of the earth on its axis is the reason, or cause, why the sun 'rises' daily." Thus, for something to be "according to reason," it must be grasped as being ultimately according to the reason in things — in the nature of things. Conversely, when something is spoken of as against reason, one means it is not only against the human capacity of that name, but fundamentally against the reason in nature and reality — the objective order, or reason, in nature which the mind grasps.

The God-given created order of reality — how God knows the world to be — undergirds the order of moral reason. Since virtue guides our conduct according to reason, when something is "against reason," in its most fundamental sense it is against virtue too.

Where does this order of nature — the "reason" for things that measures the validity and correctness of human reason — come from? It derives from the divine reason, the eternal law — an order set in things by God, their Creator. Hence when something is described as unvirtuous, this is synonymous with saying that it is against reason — the reason of God whose order placed in things constitutes nature. This is the reason or cause of their being and activity. This reason, cause, or order in things ultimately measures human reason.

Morality in the Emotions

We sometimes hear people remark that it "goes against their nature" to practice one or another moral virtue. Usually, nature in this context signifies the particular condition of one's passions or emotions. So people try to excuse themselves for unvirtuous conduct by saying, "Well, that's the way I am."

But it belongs to the perfection of moral goodness in the human person that his or her passions be governed by reason. The Catechism quotes St. Thomas Aquinas for this important teaching (1767). Other saints — St. Bonaventure, for example — could not bring themselves to believe that something so divine as graced virtue could abide in the passions, from which disordered concupiscence can also spring. Recall that concupiscence signals the effects of original sin, the primal alienation of the human person from God. Even today certain theologians explain Christian temperance and fortitude as primarily dispositions of the will that can only indirectly influence our passions or feelings.

Pagan philosophers remarked on the unruly character of sexual and other sense urges in the human person; Aristotle even suggested that they possess a life of their own. St. Paul registered a similar view concerning the power which the "law of the members" exercises in our lives (cf. Rom 7:23, 24), by which he referred to our sense appetites. As Aquinas understands the Christian life, graced — or what he called "infused" — virtue actually and directly affects these sense appetites. The infused virtues conform the unruly sense appetites to the law of reason; they form a natural part of human life and well-being. This ordering of the emotions or passions is indeed brought about by what has been called the "impression of reason" on the appetites. This is preeminently true of Christ, who had full, strong, human passions or emotions rightly ordered from within because his virtues of moderation and strengthening were so perfect in their formation.

The infused virtues of temperance and fortitude must be distinguished from the dispositions of continence and perseverance. For continence and perseverance can respectively be reduced to the sheer willing of moderation in the face of attractive things or strengthening in the face of harmful ones. Clearly in such a case the moral agent experiences interior discord, an inner struggle between the promptings of reason and the sway of disordered passion. But virtue accomplishes more than a simple truce between unruly passions and the imperatives of a duly informed will. To argue that will power alone achieves virtuous behavior is to hold out grim prospects for harmony between reason and the emotional life. Moreover, if we view the infused virtues as heroic exercises of will power, we ignore a fundamental truth concerning human sensitive appetite, namely, that the lower appetites are born to obey reason.

It is not the emotions as such but rather the effects of original and actual sin that disrupt the interior harmony of sense with reason. Hence the merely self-controlled person, while exceeding the measure of the one who loses the battle to govern the passions, falls short of the achievement of virtue: for virtue implies an inner disposition to act rightly with promptitude and joy and the accomplishment of interior wholeness with respect to the good.

By contrast the vices constitute disordered *habitus*, or dispositions, which embody patterns of behavior that disfigure the Godly image in man. Although virtue develops an integrated character, vices reduce the self to a disorganized state of fragmented potential. The practice of Christian virtue does not entail a repression of sense urges, but orders them according to the mind of Christ. The infused virtues belong to the life of Christ-centered faith, hope, and charity. For the Christian believer, this desire for a virtuous life is realized only within the context of living by faith in Christ. "He is not weak toward you, but powerful in you" (II Cor 13:3). In one who believes in him, Christ supplies the full measure of virtue, "for he was crucified out of weakness, but he lives by the power of God" (II Cor 13:4). And, therefore, neither deformity of appetite nor weakness of intellect can frustrate the power of Christ in our lives.

Moral Conscience and the Church

Christian moral teaching, as embodied in the Catechism, supposes that human actions possess a specific moral form realized by the proper configuration of object, end, and circumstance. Reasonable actions have a formative impact on the acting person by the very fact that he or she performs them. Just as a diet of pebbles can never promote good health, so morally bad actions or vices can never produce a happy person.

Christ made each of his members free so that they could find their perfection in him. "For the law of the spirit of life in Christ Jesus has freed you from the law of sin and death" (Rom 8:2). While an impaired freedom or erroneous judgment of individual conscience may excuse an individual from a measure of responsibility, these subjective factors cannot alleviate the harmful effects that such bad actions cause to integral human fulfillment. To take a practical example, a variety of circumstances may suggest depreciated moral responsibility in a teenager who engages in masturbation, yet the reduction of personal culpability does not alter the impairment of his or her ability to develop mature human communication. Habitual autoerotic behavior produces such impairment as its own punishment.

Exaggerated claims about the mind's ability to shape reality and to give "moral meaning" to concrete moral goods lead to an overemphasis on human autonomy. Unfortunately, such mental gymnastics in matters of morality ill serve the Christian call to perfection. The authority of conscience rests on moral truth, not on individual preferences or subjective views about what is good.

The pragmatic spirit behind compromising moral theologies becomes apparent when an effort is made to justify bad moral actions on the basis of alleged beneficial results and by appeal to the rights of an individual's conscience. If the development of the godly image constitutes an intrinsic perfection for the individual, extrinsic factors such as an action's likely results are not the first criteria for conscience. In fact, to argue so ignores or minimizes the effect that a vicious action produces, once the bad choice marks the character of the sinner. Even an erroneous conscience creates an obstacle to the realization of charity within the communion of the Church. "It is possible that the evil done as the result of invincible ignorance or a non-culpable error of judgment may not be imputable to the agent; but even in this case it does not cease to be an evil, a disorder in relation to truth about the good" (VS, 63).

The Declaration on Religious Liberty, *Dignitatis humanae* (no. 14), offers the best advice on the matter of moral truth and conscience: "In forming their consciences the faithful must pay careful attention to the sacred and certain teaching of the Church. For the Catholic Church is by the will of Christ the teacher of truth. It is her duty to proclaim and teach with authority the truth which is Christ and, at the same time, to declare and confirm by her authority the principles of the moral order which spring from human nature itself."

Chapter 16

Virtue and Vice

CATECHISM OF THE CATHOLIC CHURCH ¶1803 - ¶1845

Christian believers more frequently are warned to avoid sin than they are encouraged to practice virtue. A number of factors, historical and otherwise, have caused this imbalance in presenting the Christian moral tradition. But nowadays, even secular thinkers have begun to show interest in virtue. Of course, political virtue easily develops into either the heroic virtues of Homer or the pragmatic virtues of Benjamin Franklin. The saints point us in an entirely different direction.

Christian Virtue

In his Rule, St. Benedict explains how the development of virtue shapes the Christian character: "Now therefore after ascending all these steps of humility, the monk will quickly arrive at the 'perfect love' of God which 'casts out fear' (I Jn 4:18). Through this love all that he once performed with dread he will now begin to observe without effort, as though naturally, from habit, no longer out of fear of hell, but out of love for Christ, good habit, and delight in virtue. All this the Lord will by the Holy Spirit graciously manifest in his workmen now cleansed of vices and sins." When he makes living the Christian life center on the practice of virtues, St. Benedict means the infused or Christian virtues. In a similar way, the Catechism describes Christian life as a pattern of "habitual and firm disposition to do good" (1833), one which helps us to observe the Ten Commandments.

When it comes to expressing God's love for human beings, the scriptural authors rarely use juridical concepts and language, for such terms ill suit talking about the divine intimacy. Instead, the New Testament prefers images such as the Vine and the Branches (Jn 15:1-11) or the Good Shepherd (Jn 10:11-18). These parables remind us that the

Christian life finds both its origin and its direction in the person of Jesus, who is our way to God. By encouraging the practice of virtue, St. Benedict did not intend of course to exempt his monks from keeping the commandments. He does, however, insist that the monk who keeps the commandments must also manifest "good habit and delight in virtue." Good habit and delight in acting describe the internal state of the virtuous person. In commenting on the psalm verse, "Let them exult and rejoice" (cf. Ps 35:27), St. Thomas Aquinas explains that "the fruit of the saints is enjoyment because 'delight' expresses 'dilatation' of the heart and so signifies that joy is interior."

The Catechism presents an intrinsic moral theology, one that takes full account of the inner conditions that promote doing the good thing and making the right decisions. Moral commands and precepts, it is true, provide external direction for human actions. But without an intrinsic shaping of the powers and capacities from which all human action flows, no one can experience the "good habit and delight in virtue" that St. Benedict says characterizes those in whom perfect love has cast out all fear. The saints tell us that the "goal of a virtuous life is to become like God" (1803; St. Gregory of Nyssa).

Virtues and Habits

What is a virtue? According to St. Thomas, "Virtue is a good quality of mind, by which one lives righteously, of which no one can make bad use, which God works in us without us." Because this definition identifies the four main elements of virtue, the theological tradition acknowledges it as an adequate one: "A virtue is an habitual and firm disposition to do the good" which divine grace purifies and elevates (1803).

According to this definition, the exercise of virtue results only in the embrace of good objects. We cannot include every good moral object in the definition of virtue, but we can formally signal that the general character of virtue includes the realization of all moral goodness. This moral goodness concerns the whole universe of moral objects, including the supreme Object of all human pursuit and energy.

End, not environment, dominates the Christian moral life. The difference between virtue and vice lies precisely in an ordering to an end. Bad moral *habitus* or vice abuses the proper purpose of a human power and misses the mark of human flourishing, whereas good moral *habitus* or virtue observes the proper purpose of a human power or capacity and thus promotes the accomplishment of those good ends which lead to happiness. The virtues "govern our acts, order our passions, and guide our conduct in accordance with reason and faith" (1804).

Virtue does not produce boring uniformity. Rather the Christian experiences a kind of second-nature conformity to Gospel values which makes living a Christian life prompt, joyful, and easy. Unfortunately, in modern English the term "habit" connotes wearisome routine and uncreative predictability. In order to avoid confusion, some theologians retain the Latin term *habitus* when talking about the virtues. Virtue, then, is good *habitus* or firm disposition in the human soul that renders both the person who possesses it and his or her actions good. Since the virtues inspire a thousand different ways to realize the good, good actions never produce routine. By contrast, vicious *habitus*, which inclines a person to pursue an end that does not contribute to human perfection or happiness, produces a familiarity with evil that narrows a person's creative ability to love. These are the vices, and from them come sin. After a while, all vice looks the same to the sinner. For while there are many ways to express love, there are only limited ways to hate.

Only union with the person of Christ, governed by moral guidelines, can effect a real transformation of our human capacities — of intellect, will, and the sense appetites — so that they produce virtuous behavior. The transformation which grace accomplishes establishes in the virtuous person a constant disposition toward good behavior, and from this flows spiritual joy. Moreover, the possession of virtue provides the ability to act well with promptness and facility so that all of our intellectual and emotional powers readily serve the achievement of a virtuous end. Consequently, the interior struggle between what the good requires and what my instinctive leanings incline toward manifests itself with increasingly diminished intensity.

A life of virtue means full and perfect accomplishment of the moral law. Because virtue moves us from within, it establishes a harmony between ourselves and the world of moral objects. Recall: "The object chosen morally specifies the act of willing accordingly as reason recognizes and judges it good or evil" (1758). In the Christian believer, this harmonization flows from the work of the Holy Spirit. Indeed, the whole power of the New Law lies in the grace of the Holy Spirit. Those who, in the face of any moral crisis, utter the name of Jesus empowered by the Holy Spirit receive a sweeter anointing from on high than what Moses received on Mount Sinai.

Kinds of Virtue

The Catechism distinguishes the moral virtues from the intellectual; only the former perfect the whole person. Intellectual virtues, such as geometry or the culinary art, enable the one who possesses them only to think correctly or to make something well, but they do not make the whole person as well as his or her moral choices good. The moral virtues "can be grouped around the four cardinal virtues: prudence, justice, fortitude and temperance" (1834). Moral and political philosophy discuss these human virtues.

The New Testament preaches the primacy of charity: "If I . . . have not charity," says the Apostle, "I am nothing." (1826; I Cor 13:1-4). We must then distinguish the human virtues, both moral and intellectual, from the theological virtues of faith, hope, and charity. These "have the One and Triune God for their origin, motive, and object" (1812). Like the human virtues, the theological virtues constitute actual perfections of Christian believers, which "make them capable of acting as his children and of meriting eternal life" (1813). So the theological virtues develop as gifts of God's freely-bestowed grace; nothing that we do can acquire them. The Catechism instructs about both the human and infused moral virtues and the theological virtues.

The universal call to holiness determines the reason for the existence of the infused virtues. Because we require a full psychological conformity to the goods that lead to eternal life, neither charity nor faith in themselves suffice to elevate fully our moral life to a life of full

Christian engagement. The infused moral virtues help us fulfill the injunction: "whatever is true, whatever is honorable, whatever is just, whatever is pure, whatever is lovely, whatever is gracious, if there is any excellence and if there is anything worthy of praise, think about these things" (Phil 4:8).

As we have seen, the infused virtues shape even the sensitive appetites, both irascible and concupiscible. All the capacities or powers of the rational soul belong to the acting person. Moral truth must affect every aspect of our personality, "just as it is better for someone both to will the good and to do it by an external act, so it also belongs to perfect moral good that we be moved toward the good not only through our will but also through our sense appetites, according to the saying of Psalm 84:3: 'My heart and my flesh cry out for the living God.' "

Chapter 17

The Human Community and Grace

CATECHISM OF THE CATHOLIC CHURCH ¶1877 - ¶1948

The Gospel of Christ offers us not only new life, but also a new way of life. The ideal of a community life, as recorded in the Acts of the Apostles, continues to inspire Christian believers to incarnate this model of shared values and common goals in today's world. Toward this goal, Pope John Paul II insists that we undertake a critique of modern culture, especially in the Western democracies where, the Pope insists, various factors have combined to eclipse moral truth. His encyclical *Evangelium vitae* illumines the Catechism's discussion of the human community.

The Kingdom of God and His Justice

"A society is a group of persons bound together organically by a principle of unity that goes beyond each one of them" (1880). No individual, even if he or she lives alone, escapes belonging to a group. Everyone must enjoy some form of human relationship. Because other persons exist in the world, justice constitutes a true virtue. Justice is about our relations with the other and about equality. According to St. Thomas Aquinas, "justice is a *habitus* (habit) according to which a person is said to be active by choosing what is right." This means that Christian justice is never a matter of simply knowing what is right to do, but of steadfastly accomplishing what is just and right.

The Christian notion of right is distinctive. Because all human rights find their origin in the eternal law, the Gospel affirms that there exists an objective ground for the establishment of a right. The modern notion of right as arising from what the majority decides and as guaranteed by a foundational document, such as a constitution, cannot substitute for the eternal law. Indeed, the Holy Father laments the extent to which today parliaments have wrenched rights from their objective grounds where they always serve to promote the good of the human person. He claims that this is the "sinister result of relativism which reigns unopposed: the 'right' ceases to be such, because it is no longer firmly founded on the inviolable dignity of the person, but is made subject to the will of the stronger part" (*Evangelium vitae,* 20). In this way, democracy, so the Pope concludes, effectively moves toward a form of totalitarianism.

While the application of the principles of justice requires that the just man or woman take account of actual social circumstances, we must first of all enquire about the nature of justice as a real virtue. Every interpersonal relationship develops from and involves an exchange among human persons; like any human activity, this civil congress requires a measure of virtuous regulation. But what is more important, justice forms a truly behavioral virtue. As a true *habitus* of character, justice shapes the personal capacities of a human subject so that he or she experiences the "habitual and firm disposition" to act justly in the form of an inclination.

It is wrongheaded to think that achieving justice simply requires analysis of institutional structures and social critique. For "the way in which man is involved in building his own future depends on the understanding he has of himself and of his own destiny. It is on this level that the Church's specific and decisive contribution to true culture is to be found" (*Centesimus annus*, 51). In the final analysis, the transformation of the world is accomplished in the hearts of those who accept the Gospel of truth, the Gospel of life. Since there is no concrete solution to social questions apart from the Gospel, only the believer who loves the moral good that justice embodies is ready to address alleged institutionalization of injustice. On the other hand, the person who fights for justice outside of union with Christ runs the risk of developing a vindictive spirit instead of a "hunger and thirst for righteousness" (Mt 5:6).

The Call to Social Justice

Gaudium et spes also reminds us that the cardinal virtue of justice principally concerns one of the primary givens of human experience — the fact that there are other persons in the world. Scriptural revelation in both the Old and the New Testaments speaks of an active commitment to the other — the neighbor — and demands that each of us share responsibility for all of humankind. The virtuously just person always shows an active concern for bettering the reciprocal relationships that comprise the moral universe of human society. St. Thomas Aquinas warns, however, that this pursuit is likely to fail without due attention paid to the virtues of personal discipline, such as moderation, courage, and patience.

In her call for a just social order, the Church urges us to consider the ambit of justice as coextensive with the global community of nations. Again in *Gaudium et spes*, we read: "Because of the closer bonds of human interdependence and their spread over the whole world, we are today witnessing a widening of the role of the common good, which is the sum total of social conditions which allow people, either as groups or as individuals, to reach their fulfillment more fully and more easily. The whole human race is consequently involved with regard to the rights and obligations which result" (26). The Catechism suggests that there exists a certain resemblance between the blessed Trinity and the fraternity that men ought to establish among themselves (1890).

This trinitarian perspective leads us to consider the notion of the common good. In Catholic social doctrine, the common good requires three essential elements: respect for persons; concern for social well-being, which should be concretized in a plan for development; and a reasonable security which ensures the maintenance of peace. Ordinarily, the political community is charged with preserving this common good. In order for this goal to be achieved, however, both those who bear the responsibility of civil governance and those governed require virtues so as to worthily discharge the offices of their states in life.

Social Justice and the Virtues of Civility

Since it regulates interpersonal relationships, the cardinal virtue of justice governs significant areas of human life. In addition to the ordinary forms of distributive and commutative justice, these virtues fall under two main headings: the virtues of veneration and the virtues of civility. While on the one hand, justice ordinarily aims at establishing a certain, definite equality (*ad æqualitatem*) between individuals of the same rank, justice can also extend to what transpires among non-peers. Broadly speaking then, the first group of virtues — those of *veneration* — regulates relationships between inferiors and superiors. These are the virtues of authority and personal responsibility.

But justice also covers those circumstances in the human community when the requirements established by either general justice or a form of particular justice do not pertain. The second group of virtues — those of *civility* — regulate and direct interpersonal transactions among people who share life in the same society. These virtues of civility moderate the actions of persons who share the same status and condition — peers within the larger social grouping.

However, one should not draw the distinction between the virtues of veneration and the virtues of civility too sharply. Indeed, the religious man or woman who respects authority is best prepared to manifest a civil spirit towards others.

The *virtues of civility* form two classes. First, there are virtues that are required for common life because they regulate those exchanges that are indispensable for any form of authentic human communication. Secondly, there are virtues that contribute to living a happier experience of everyday life, or that simply develop more pleasant living, without thereby constituting absolute moral prerequisites of social life.

The first group includes the virtues of truth, gratitude, and vengeance, whereas the second group includes the virtues of liberality and friendship or affability.

The first group of virtues — truth, gratitude, and vengeance — more fully realizes the essential component of justice. They regulate activities that one can recognize as legitimately due to other people. The virtue of *truth* governs "uprightness in human action and speech," indeed "showing oneself true in deeds and truthful in words" (2468). This virtue entails "honesty and discretion" (2469). The virtue of thankfulness or *gratitude* governs our recollection and acknowledgment of benefactions. The virtue of *vengeance* — whose name should not lead one to confuse it with the disordered vindictiveness that the term might be taken to connote — controls the measure and kind of self-defense and retribution called for by harm done to oneself, to a friend, or to persons in one's care. It is indeed the deprivation of this virtue which is discernible in pure vindictiveness pursued for emotional reasons. This virtue is similarly lacking to those who turn a blind eye toward vicious conduct, failing to protect against and penalize it. The virtue of vengeance involves foresight to frustrate, and prudent chastening to deter, acts destructive of civil amity and peace. Such a virtue is a mean between the extremes of indifference and passivity toward evil on the one hand, and unthinking vindictiveness and dangerous aggression on the other.

Among the second group of virtues pertinent to civility — those which enhance the joys of social life — one finds the *habitus* of *friendliness*. It is the virtue of friendliness, rather than a quarrelsome or meretricious spirit, that makes life within the human community more pleasant and joyful. Likewise, it is liberality rather than an avaricious or prodigal spirit that measures the right manner of acquitting oneself of debts that form no part of strict justice. These moral virtues might indeed be described by the words of Edmund Burke, "the unbought grace of life," for they make of our comings and goings in society a tapestry of small pleasures and joys innocently and charitably given and received.

The gift of the Holy Spirit that aids justice is *piety*. St. Thomas Aquinas explains its special significance when he observes that this gift illumines the just believer to embrace every person, and indeed everything, as a child or possession of the heavenly Father. This gift accordingly brings to an evangelical perfection whatever remains of the juridical and limited in the exercise of justice, thereby transforming in a mysterious way this heaven and this earth into the new heavens and the new earth (Rev 21:1). This returns us to the theme of the Godly image which controls the moral teaching of the Catechism. "The vocation of humanity is to show forth the image of God and to be transformed into the image of the Father's only Son" (1877).

Chapter 18

Law and Grace

CATECHISM OF THE CATHOLIC CHURCH ¶1949 - ¶2051

The Gospel of Grace represents the final victory of Christ's saving work. Unfortunately, morality is too often preached outside of the context of the transformed life. Hence the impression is easily given that good deeds, instead of flowing from the justified believer, are the price one pays to gain access to the intimacy of the trinitarian life. But since justification includes the remission of sins, sanctification, and the renewal of the inner man, keeping the commandments actually perfects human freedom, making us more and more lovers of neighbor and God.

Providence and the Eternal Law

The theme of God's wisdom enjoys a prominent place in the Scriptures. St. Paul exclaims, "Rather we speak God's wisdom, mysterious, hidden, which God predetermined before the ages for our glory" (I Cor 2:7). As a wise Father, God offers us a fatherly instruction that leads to beatitude.

Quoting St. Augustine, St. Thomas Aquinas reminds us that the "law which is named the supreme reason cannot be otherwise understood than as unchangeable and eternal." Eternal law is thus the permanent expression of God's wisdom and embodies the "ruling idea, the *ratio*, of all things which exist in God as the effective sovereign of them all."

The Catechism, then, associates eternal law with God's providence for the world; the order of divine government directly flows from the eternal law (1954). This divine *ordo rerum,* or order of things, undergirds the whole of the created moral order; in short, eternal law represents how God knows the world to be, how he effectively conceives the ordering of everything that exists within creation. Within this order, the human person, aided by law, freely chooses to pursue a life of love and service.

The term "law" includes a wide range of meanings; as one author puts it, "from the pure and eternal exemplar in the mind of God to the unsteady beat of lust in human nature." The common note which allows for the broadly analogical deployment of the term law centers on the notion of regulation: the natural moral law, the Old Law, the New Law or the Law of the Gospel, and civil and ecclesiastical laws. In these instances, the ordinance of reason is manifested in diverse, but harmonious, ways. Since the moral law finds its fullness and its unity in Christ, and no genuine human law can frustrate the eternal law, civil law must exist in conformity with the moral law (1953). For we have here no earthly dwelling, but await the new heavens and the new earth.

The New Law of Grace and Freedom

Only the grace of the Holy Spirit given inwardly to those who are united with Christ accomplishes the justification proper to the Christian dispensation. Nothing else, including the very words of Scripture themselves, can directly and immediately cause this freely-bestowed divine action within the human creature. Everything the Church uses to communicate grace is an instrument: the Creed, the Ten Commandments, other doctrines proposed for our belief, the sacraments. Of course, all of these serve a purpose for promoting the New Law, but none of them possesses the ability by itself of transforming the human person into a son or daughter of the Lord. "Thus even the Gospel letter kills unless the healing grace of faith is present within." The First Letter of John teaches: "And his commandment is this: we should believe in the name of his Son, Jesus Christ, and love one another just as he has commanded us. Those who keep his commandments remain in him, and he in them, and the way we know that he remains in us is from the Spirit that he gave" (I Jn 3: 23, 24). The New Law, then, is called a law of love, of grace, and of freedom.

St. Thomas Aquinas gives a short, but very accurate account of the Church's teaching on law and freedom: "The New Law is called the law of freedom in two senses. First, because it does not constrain us to do or to avoid anything apart from what of itself is necessary or contrary to salvation, falling under the precept or the prohibition of the law. Secondly, because even such precepts or prohibitions it makes us fulfill freely, as much as we fulfill them by an inner stirring of grace. For these two reasons the New Law is called the law of perfect freedom."

Still, a question remains: What good deeds must one do in order to inherit eternal life (cf. Mt 19:16)? In other words, does the New Law sufficiently regulate external actions?

The Church includes the sacraments and the commandments among the externals of the New Law. She further teaches that, in addition to the seven sacraments of the New Law, "those moral precepts which of themselves are formally implied in virtuous action sufficiently regulate our external comportment." The detailed, even meticulous, legislation of the Old Law surrenders to the reign of grace which "is rightly exercised by works of charity." There is something distinctive about Christian morality, for the bestowal of divine grace properly belongs to the Gospel dispensation. And divine grace alone accounts for the existence of the infused virtues, which are distinctively those which derive from participation in the Christian mysteries.

St. Thomas writes: "Now it is the grace of the Holy Spirit, given through faith in Christ, which is predominant in the law of the New Covenant, and that in which its whole power consists." This teaching forms the heart of the Catechism's interpretation of Christian justification and the new life that flows from it. For from the moment the Holy Spirit dwells in the believer, the Christian possesses the capacity, realized primarily in the virtue of prudence, to make the moral decisions required for a holy life. Likewise the Holy Spirit provides the rectitude of emotion and appetite — especially in the infused moral virtues and the allied Gifts of the Holy Spirit — which sets the believer in motion toward the authentic goods of human fulfillment and beatitude. All those who are justified in the blood of Christ receive the life of the Holy Spirit, who breathes charity into them and who forms them into the Body of Christ, which is the Church.

The Spirit in the Church

"When the Advocate comes whom I will send you from the Father, the Spirit of truth that proceeds from the Father, he will testify to me" (Jn 15:26). God has freely chosen to associate man with the work of his grace. So Christ's promise that the Holy Spirit abides in the Church guarantees that we, Christ's members, can both know the truth and live it. The Christian believer, then, is called to practice the "truth of life," and can be said to merit the reward of eternal life. Like anything else, one's life is called true on the basis of its reaching its rule and norm, namely divine or eternal law. By conforming to God's truth, our lives possess the uprightness of the just. This kind of truth, our rectitude, remains common to every virtue.

The Holy Spirit provides both the law of virtuous living and the virtue itself to those who heed his promptings. Neither the many complexities of daily life nor the sometimes unruly power of human emotion constitute obstacles to the effectiveness of the divine power in the life of the believer. The whole of the Christian dispensation, especially the sacramental life of the Church, aims toward the creation of a new people who, by their holy lives, offer a pleasing sacrifice to the Lord. "The children of our holy mother the Church rightly hope *for the grace of final perseverance and the recompense* of God their Father for the good works accomplished with his grace in communion with Jesus" (2016).

Within the pilgrim Church, a dynamic interplay between sin and forgiveness characterizes the Christian moral life. St. Augustine summarizes the unfolding of truth in the Christian life: "From the law comes knowledge of sin, by faith the reception of grace against sin, by grace the soul is healed of the imperfection of sin; a healthy soul possesses freedom of choice; freedom of choice is ordered to love of righteousness; love of righteousness is the accomplishment of the law."

The Church proclaims the holiness of Christ as the sole source for a Godly life. Moreover, Jesus himself instructs us that there is no moment in our lives when sin provides an excuse for turning away from God. For when one of the criminals who was crucified with Jesus, turned to him and said " 'Jesus, remember me when you come into your kingdom,' he replied to him, 'Amen, I say to you, today you will be with me in Paradise' " (Lk 23:42, 43). The truth about God's love for the sinner and the transformation which occurs in the lives of all those who seek to do God's will must accompany every instruction about morality. Failure to pay heed to these truths results in a gross perversion of the basic New Testament teaching about the divine love, namely, that God loves us, not because we are good, but because he is goodness itself.

The Church is called mother and teacher because she fulfills the twofold task of instructing us about the truth of life and communicating to us the grace that we need to observe the commandments and practice the virtues. The magisterium of the pastors of the Church remains, indispensably, at the very heart of the Church's teaching office. We should ask for the grace to develop a true filial spirit of piety toward the Church, so that we can appreciate more and more the lavish gifts of God's Word and of the body and blood of God's Son that we receive daily from the altars of the world. From this Eucharistic communion we receive the strength for every good that we should do and the patience to sustain whatever evil we must endure.

Chapter 19

Moral Precepts and the Commandments of Love

CATECHISM OF THE CATHOLIC CHURCH ¶2052 - ¶2195

The Decalogue

Since the earliest days of the Church, the Ten Commandments have occupied a predominant place in the catechesis given to Christian believers. According to the divinely-warranted assurance recorded in the book of Deuteronomy, the Decalogue or "ten words" point the way to a full and happy life: "If you obey the commandments of the Lord, your God, which I enjoin on you today, loving him, and walking in his ways, and keeping his commandments, statutes and decrees, you will live and grow numerous" (Dt 30:16). The Old Testament always locates the Ten Commandments within the memory and the promise of the Exodus, the event which stands out at the center of the Old Covenant as God's great liberating deed.

The Exodus captures the Christian imagination. St. Augustine teaches that the life of the people of the Exodus "foretold and prefigured Christ." This further implies that the keeping of the precepts of the Old Law actually disposed the human race to receive the justifying grace of Christ. And so Christians believe that the Ten Commandments receive their "full meaning" (2056) only in the New Covenant, which is written in the blood of Christ, "the Lamb that was slain" (Rev 5:12).

The Ten Commandments are the prime principles in the whole of God's law. One of the first Church theologians, St. Irenaeus of Lyons, recognized that the Ten Commandments comprise a comprehensive list of moral instruction that, in principle, lies open to human inquiry. This does not suggest, however, that the Ten Commandments offer fair game for any kind of philosophical revisionism. Rather the Decalogue embodies the truth about human life and right conduct that God himself has made part of his plan of creation. So the Catechism makes a point of associating the Ten Commandments with the natural moral law: "The Decalogue contains a privileged expression of the natural law. It is made known to us by divine revelation and by human reason" (2080).

To be sure, the saints remind us that a sinful human race required God's special revelation in order to possess a full explanation of the Decalogue. What St. Thomas Aquinas calls the "secondary precepts" of the natural law — "conclusions following closely from first principles" — needed to be repromulgated by God to pierce the disorienting veil of sin afflicting humanity. Yet, were the first precepts of the natural law not immune from destruction, men and women could not recognize the teaching of the Decalogue in its true nature. Hence, these general principles of the natural law, in the abstract, cannot be blotted out from men's hearts. Christian tradition has always affirmed that God has implanted in man the knowledge of the precepts contained in the Decalogue. The natural law is promulgated in creation, and repromulgated in privileged fashion in the precepts of the Decalogue: precepts that embody the actual intention of the lawgiver who is God himself.

Thus the Ten Commandments nourish and sustain both reason and faith. The Catechism quotes St. Irenaeus to explain that "from the beginning, God had implanted in the heart of man the precepts of the natural law. Then he was content to remind him of them. This was the Decalogue" (2070). In other words, the Ten Commandments represent moral truth dictated by reason which itself is informed by faith.

For this reason, our judgments about the structure of human nature and about the rightness of our actions have authority only in so far as they conform to standards that are independent of judgment, desire, choice, and will. These are standards of truth as well as of rational justification. From the fact that the ultimate criteria for moral conduct come from God, and "by natural generation nor by human choice nor by a man's decision but of God" (Jn 1:13), we can conclude that the Decalogue does not constitute an optional code of conduct destined only to guide the consciences of religious believers. Rather, the Ten Commandments contain moral truth that is indispensable for the happiness and well-being of every member of the human race. For this reason, the precepts directed to the preservation of the common good, or the order of justice and virtue admit of no dispensation whatsoever, including the always attractive option of self-dispensation.

This datum opens an important window on the quest of some contemporaries to stipulate a definition for the temporal "common good" that is wholly separated from either virtue or reverence for God. Such a view of the common good being founded upon fiction, it can lead only to social disarray and moral harm.

The Two Tables of the Law

As we learn from the account recorded in Exodus, the Ten Commandments were handed over to Moses on tablets of stone (cf. Ex 24:12). Christian catechesis accordingly speaks about two tablets or tables of the Old Law. Recall that Moses is said to have carried down two tablets from Mount Sinai, which God had inscribed with words of the covenant (cf. Ex 34:29). The precepts of the first table, which direct the human creature's thoughts, words, and deeds toward God, stipulate the right ordering of the human race to God himself — our ultimate Good. The precepts of the second table prescribe for our dealings with one another and embody the order of justice which should prevail in dealings both with our superiors and among our peers.

The Catechism treats the first table under a heading drawn from Christ's own words as recorded in Matthew 22:37, "You shall love the Lord, your God, with all your heart, with all your soul, and with all your mind." The Catechism's treatment of the first three commandments occupies twenty-five pages. The consideration of the second table — entitled, "You shall love your neighbor as yourself" (Mt 22:39) — takes up the eighty-pages of chapter two. The titles of these two chapters remind us that Christian doctrine considers all authentic moral precepts as ordered toward the fulfillment of the great commandment of charity. "The commandments of the Decalogue," says St. Thomas Aquinas, "have as their end the love of God and of neighbor."

Since the Ten Commandments lead to the virtue of charity, Christ himself not only teaches the commandments but also fulfills them. He does this in his very own person. The Gospel teaches us that our Blessed Savior fulfilled the moral precepts when he suffered out of love for his Father and out of love for his neighbor. St. Paul expresses the concrete application of this mystery when he writes to the Galatians: "As I now live in the flesh, I live by faith in the Son of God, who has loved me and given himself up for me" (Gal 2:20). As the priest appointed to serve on our behalf, Christ restored and perfected the order of justice in humankind's relations with God. Apart from Christ's redemptive sacrifice, the commandments would only strike terror in the hearts of those who heard them: revealing the wretchedness of the human condition before the inviolate majesty and purity of the divine law. But because of Calvary, Christ's true worship of God has opened up a way for divine love and mercy to express itself in the world.

The Commandments and Religion

The first three commandments, the commandments of the first table, teach us about actions that belong specifically to the virtue of religion. In the schema of the virtues, religion falls under the *ratio* of the cardinal virtue of justice, forming its most important part. St. Thomas Aquinas explains why these commandments lay the foundation for the whole Christian life. "The person who is to be built up in virtue through law," he explains, "must first, as it were, lay the foundation of religion, whereby the human creature is set in proper relationship to God, who is the final end of all human willing." This virtue is at root natural while being uplifted in the grace of God.

I am the Lord your God: you shall not have strange gods before me. The Roman Catechism taught that the first commandment embraces the theological virtues of faith, hope, and charity. Since God has revealed his glory to us, we are bound to seek the truth about God and confess it with heart and lips. Then we are bound to hope for our salvation by trusting God's omnipotent mercy, and, above all, to maintain an undivided heart in loving the One who is the source of every good thing. The first commandment ensures that our hearts become one with the heart of Christ, so that we can pray the prayer that Christ himself taught us. "Our Father in heaven, / hallowed be your name" (Mt 6:9). The commandment reminds us of our status as God's children, who, like merchants in search of fine pearls, are ready to sacrifice everything for the "pearl of great price" (Mt 13:46).

"Him alone shall you serve" (Lk 4:8). So Jesus instructs his disciples. The first commandment instructs us about adoration, prayer, sacrifice — the ways we express the virtue of religion. It also warns us against various practices whereby we can be tempted to worship false gods: superstition, idolatry, giving credence to divination, and indulging in magical spells, and flirting with the sorcerer's deception. The first commandment also condemns the sins against religion itself: tempting God, which is an expression of doubt about his love, his providence, or his power; sacrilege; and simony, which is the unlawful buying or selling of spiritual goods.

You shall not take the name of the Lord your God in vain. The second commandment instructs us about the reverence due to the holy name of God. The Old Testament teaches us that the name reveals the mystery of the person who bears it. "The name is the icon of the person" (2158). Throughout the Christian centuries, holy men and women have pondered the mystery of the names of God, of our blessed Savior, and of the saints, especially the Queen of All Saints. Their meditation reflects the New Testament command that instructs us to venerate the name of Jesus, "the name that is above every name" (Phil 2:9) and helps us recognize the seriousness of blasphemy, the utterance of hateful, reproachful, or defiant words against God, his angels, and his saints.

Remember to keep holy the Lord's Day. "The Sunday celebration of the Lord's Day and his Eucharist is at the heart of the Church's life" (2177; CIC, can. 1246, 1). This final commandment of the first table of the Decalogue regulates the observance of the Sunday sabbath, which the Catechism calls "a day of grace and rest from work." Our participation in the Holy Sacrifice of the Mass makes us share in the perfect worship that Christ offers to the Father. This worship not only satisfies in a preeminent way the obligation incumbent on every creature to worship and reverence the Creator; it also, and further, perfects us as children of God and coheirs with Christ. Through our Eucharistic communion with the Lord, we grow in filial piety, the virtue that teaches us to reverence everyone as children of the Heavenly Father and to respect everything as his possession. So when we leave the Eucharistic assembly, we are prepared to fulfill the solemn command that Jesus once gave to his disciples, "Love one another. As I have loved you, so you should love one another" (Jn 13:34).

Chapter 20

Commandments and Virtues

CATECHISM OF THE CATHOLIC CHURCH ¶2197 - ¶2550

"Owe nothing to anyone, except to love one another; for the one who loves another has fulfilled the law" (Rom 13:8). St. Thomas Aquinas insists that the commandments of the Decalogue have as their end the love of God and of neighbor. More specifically, the commandments of the second table instruct us about the kind of actions that preserve the order of justice and virtue in the world of human conduct. The Catechism continues the venerated custom of the Church which employs the Ten Commandments as the basis for moral instruction. This practice became formalized in the moralists and catechists of the sixteenth-century Reformation and Counter-Reformation and continues to provide an organizational structure for practical moral teaching.

Virtues and the Commandments

St. Thomas Aquinas and other saints and theologians before and after him exemplify a different and complementary approach. Their approach to the moral life focuses on the actual strengths necessary for one to live the life prescribed by the Decalogue. They do not compose their moral theology around the Ten Commandments as key points but prefer to speak about the virtues. This alternative model takes the cardinal or "hinge" moral virtues of prudence, justice, fortitude, and temperance as the main headings under which to discuss the whole matter of Christian morality.

In the Christian life the cardinal virtues are further ordered toward the final end of union with God. Hence no complete account of the cardinal virtues is possible without reference to the theological virtues of faith, hope, and charity, which perfect the believer by uniting him or her directly to God. In the actual order of providence, God has uplifted human nature to a share in his own uncreated life through sanctifying grace and charity. Thus the natural virtues are vivified, uplifted, and redirected toward God himself — an infinitely higher object and end than any finite good. Hence even the smallest acts of virtue now may express God's own love. Any act of generosity or goodness may embody not only what is naturally fitting and good but also, through that seed of eternal life which is charity, the very supernatural love of the Trinity.

Of course the virtues are related to the commandments of the Decalogue; they are needed to live the Decalogue. St. Thomas Aquinas, for example, teaches that each one of the commandments of the second table expresses variously the requirements of the virtue of justice. This is especially true in the case of the first of these commandments which prescribes that we pay the honor of reverence to our parents.

The divine wisdom is manifest in the ordering of the Ten Commandments. The fourth commandment, *Honor your father and your mother*, comes right after the commandments that establish us in a proper relationship to God. Why? Parents are the immediate source of existence for us, and so they share in God's creative power in a distinctive way. Pope John Paul II points this out when he teaches that conjugal love, which itself is a gift to spouses, "does not end with the couple, because it makes them capable of the greatest possible gift, the gift by which they become cooperators with God for giving life to a new human person" (*Familiaris consortio,* 14). St. Thomas Aquinas put it this way: "Under God we hold the blessing of physical existence from our parents."

The fourth commandment strikingly illustrates the relationship between the moral order and the order that we discover in the universe. Natural law "refers to man's proper and primordial nature, the 'nature of the human person,' which is the person himself in the unity of soul and body, in the unity of his spiritual and biological inclinations and of all the other specific characteristics necessary for the pursuit of his end" (VS, 50 citing GS, 51).

Christian moral teaching recognizes in the divine ordering — indeed, in the law — of human procreation, the very foundation of the moral duties of family members toward one another, especially of children toward their parents. While the debt to parents has precedence over that to country and kin, still the justice of the fourth commandment also directs us to demonstrate piety toward our country, its officials, and kinfolk. The connection is natural and therefore obvious: by being born of our parents, these relatives and this homeland become ours.

The Negative Precepts of the Decalogue

The virtues constitute stable positive qualities in the person that enable one to do the good promptly, joyfully, easily, and well. By contrast, the last six commandments comprise negative precepts that forbid inflicting harm on our neighbor. Hence the remaining commandments of the Decalogue are only indirectly linked with a positive account of the virtues. Rather, these final six commandments target and prohibit the chief forms of injustice toward one's neighbor. The second table of the Decalogue contains six negative precepts: the fifth commandment, *You shall not kill*; the sixth commandment, *You shall not commit adultery*; the seventh commandment, *You shall not steal*; the eighth commandment, *You shall not bear false witness against your neighbor*; the ninth commandment, *You shall not covet your neighbor's wife*; the tenth commandment, *You shall not covet your neighbor's goods*. As St. Thomas Aquinas puts it, all of the "injuries that can be afflicted upon neighbors come down to the matters proscribed here, which are the more universal and the more urgent." To express this in a positive way, these commandments ensure that we fulfill St. Paul's injunction to the Romans: "Pay to all their due" (Rom 13:7).

The encyclical letter of Pope John Paul II, *Veritatis splendor*, which was issued after the publication of the Catechism, sets forth a number of actions that in one sense or another may be categorized as moral injustices. The following examples illustrate bad actions that contradict the good of the person made in God's image. The list is taken from *Gaudium et spes* (27): "Whatever is hostile to life itself, such as any kind of homicide, genocide, abortion, euthanasia and voluntary suicide; whatever violates the integrity of the human person, such as mutilation, physical and mental torture and attempts to coerce the spirit;

whatever is offensive to human dignity, such as subhuman living conditions, arbitrary imprisonment, deportation, slavery, prostitution and trafficking in women and children; degrading conditions of work which treat laborers as mere instruments of profit, and not as free responsible persons: all these and the like are a disgrace, and so long as they infect human civilization they contaminate those who inflict them more than those who suffer injustice. Further, they are a negation of the honor due to the Creator" (VS, 80).

This passage is not meant to provide an exhaustive listing of all intrinsically evil acts. However, it does give contemporary illustration of conduct incapable of being ordered to God and to the good of the person. It is fitting that negative precepts forbidding injustice to one's neighbor are listed among the Ten Commandments. The human race needs to know the things that impede the good of the human person and, therefore, thwart the development of the human community.

And so Pope John Paul II reaffirms the Church's teaching that one may never choose the kinds of behavior expressed in negative form in the Old and New Testaments. "The negative precepts of the natural law are universally valid. They oblige each and every individual, always and in every circumstance. It is a matter of prohibitions which forbid a given action *semper et pro semper,* without exception, because the choice of this kind of behavior is in no way compatible with the goodness of the will of the acting person, with his vocation to life with God and to communion with his neighbor" (VS, 52). With magisterial authority, the Pope glosses the teaching that St. Paul gave to the Romans, "Love does no evil to the neighbor; hence, love is the fulfillment of the law" (Rom 13:10).

Virtues, Commandments, and Growth in the Spirit

Yet for the Christian it is not sufficient to avoid transgressions against the well-being of our neighbor. We are called upon to perform corporal and spiritual works of mercy. These include a large variety of positive services that can be rendered to our neighbor. But as St. Thomas Aquinas explains, no adequate account of them could be set down in the Decalogue, "for it is not possible to frame common affirmative precepts about, say, temperance, for its exercise varies according to different times and according to diverse laws and human customs."

Here one discerns how the account of the cardinal virtues (prudence, temperance, fortitude, justice) and the theological virtues (faith, hope, and charity) provides the context to understand spiritual growth. One prays and strives to develop virtue so as not to fall beneath that minimal threshold of charity indicated by the final six negative precepts of the Decalogue — but virtue is ordered far beyond this minimal threshold. One needs virtue not merely to avoid sin (and surmount obstacles), but to enable one to move powerfully and joyously toward the ends of a good life — to blossom in enacting the love of God and neighbor. The moral virtues aid the moralist and the catechist to enumerate in concrete and specific ways the right way to fulfill the commandment of love.

The "Doctor of Love," St. Thérèse of Lisieux, like a watchful sister, has a helpful word for us as we face so many virtues and commandments: "Ah! Lord, I know you don't command the impossible. You know better than I do my weakness and imperfection; You know very well that never would I be able to love my Sisters as You love them, unless *You*, O my Jesus, loved them in me. It is because You wanted to give me this grace that You made Your new commandment. Oh! how I love this new commandment since it gives me the assurance that Your Will is to love in me all those You command me to love! Yes, I feel it, when I am charitable, it is Jesus alone who is acting in me, and the more united I am to Him, the more do I love."

Chapter 21

The Moment of Communion: Why Do We Need to Pray?

If Almighty God, who created us and sustains us in being, already knows our every need, why is it necessary for Christians to pray? In his *Confessions,* St. Augustine noted: "If a person confesses to you, Lord, he does not reveal his inmost thoughts to you as though you did not know them." Our prayer in no way informs or enlightens God. That is not prayer's point.

And yet, as the Catechism reminds us, prayer remains a vital necessity in the life of every believer. "If we do not allow the Spirit to lead us [through prayer], we fall back into the slavery of sin. How can the Holy Spirit be our life if our heart is far from him? . . . Prayer and *Christian life* are *inseparable*" (2744, 2745). Prayer, then, is the way that we keep our heart close to God.

Therefore, before exploring the Christian tradition's three major expressions of prayer — vocal, meditative, and contemplative — it is helpful to consider the general and very practical question of why we need to pray. There are seven reasons that reflect the seminal insight of the Catechism.

Prayer Keeps Us Mindful of Our Spiritual Nature

The materialism and sensuality of the world readily cause us to forget our spiritual essence. It drags us down, luring us into a false contentment that is governed by self-indulgence and selfishness. Worldliness undermines the humility and detachment essential to authentic holiness. It damages our self-knowledge, deadens our sense of dignity, and destroys our chances for self-perfection.

The spiritual act of prayer comes to our rescue by recharging our spiritual self, which otherwise stagnates. By looking beyond our carnal wants and needs, beyond the venal cravings of the world, prayer focuses our hearts and minds on the glory of God and the beauty of sanctity. It makes us long for the good things that really make all the difference in our life.

Prayer Enables Us to Surrender Our Will to God

Perhaps the principal obstacle to our growth in grace is our own prideful willfulness. It is not easy to turn over our desires, to give up our ambitions and to relinquish control in our life. The Lord was keenly aware of this struggle in us for, when teaching his disciples to pray to the Father, he instructed them to implore: "Thy will be done" (Mt 6:10).

We need to pray that every day, for doing God's will is not always easy, especially when our own will seems so much more suitable. The filter of prayer constantly clarifies what is truly good and fitting for us. Aided by prayer, our will then goes after divine goodness with great gusto, averting all the false and deceptive goods that clamor for our attention. Through the agency of prayer, our own willfulness decreases as our souls become more perfectly conformed to the will of God in which we take unbounded delight.

Prayer Purifies and Empowers Human Freedom

Like all of our human powers, freedom itself must be formed and developed through our spiritual union with Jesus. As the Catechism points out, "Human freedom . . . attains its perfection when directed toward God, our beatitude. . . .The more one does what is good, the freer one becomes. There is no true freedom except in the service of what is good and just" (1731, 1733).

Prayer, which directs our heart, soul, mind, and strength to God, in turn directs our freedom toward God. It fills us with joy over our God-centered choices. Prayer equips us to live freely in the truth by orienting us to Jesus, the Way, the Truth, and the Life.

Prayer Enlightens Our Self-knowledge

The first step in reaching holiness is the acknowledgment of our personal need for mercy brought on by our sins. However, as the Catechism makes clear, "Without the knowledge Revelation gives of God we cannot recognize sin clearly" (387). The way we come to share in the knowledge of divine Revelation is precisely through prayer. Therefore, as Christians we rely on prayer to help us know our self-centered ways, and to turn them over to God confidently in the grace of his Spirit.

Prayer Disposes Us to Receive Divine Gifts

God, who "never ceases to draw man to himself" (27), created man "to make him share in his own blessed life" (1). But we need to be open and supple in order to accept the graces that bless us with a sharing in God's divine life. Prayer provides that spiritual preparation. It conditions and sensitizes us to the things of God so that we can respond to them promptly, easily, joyfully.

Without prayer we become callous and closed in on ourselves. Spiritual things seem superfluous to us. We become haughty, dismissive, and presumptuous toward the things of God. But prayer makes us attentive, watchful, and alert. It generates in us a holy anticipation to participate in even the slightest and most subtle offerings of God's Holy Spirit. It attunes us to the truth that sometimes God reveals himself in wisps and whispers.

Prayer Fulfills Our Highest Vocation

The Catechism instructs us that man "is 'the only creature on earth that God has willed for its own sake,' and he alone is called to share, by knowledge and love, in God's own life. It was for this end that he was created, and this is the fundamental reason for his dignity" (356; GS, 24).

Through ardent prayer, that God-given dignity is realized. Human beings were made to pray. So often we are tempted to discount prayer as a meaningless waste of time. We wonder what good can come of it . . . shouldn't we be doing something more concrete and practical? Yet heartfelt prayer effects more good in us and in others than we can ever know. It is the source of our self-fulfillment. It expands us, and perfects us, and completes us. In prayer we experience true communion with the saints and angels . . . a foretaste of the eternal beatitude of heaven.

Prayer Unites Us to God

The Catechism tells us that prayer is "a vital and personal relationship with the living and true God" from which we live out the mystery of faith (2558). People have many misconceived ideas about how we can connect with God. But, as one classic spiritual author reassures us, "by love God may be touched and embraced, never by thought." It takes more than rational notions and concepts to bond with God. For the Lord longs to be one with us through the union of hearts. Prayer of the heart accomplishes that union.

In making us one with God, holy prayer also repairs our inner disharmony and restores our integrity. And in so doing, prayer serves the designs of God's Providence. To close with the words of St. Catherine of Siena: "The medicine by which God willed to heal the whole world is humble, constant, holy prayer."

Chapter 22

Vocal Prayer

CATECHISM OF THE CATHOLIC CHURCH ¶2700 - ¶2704

Whenever we hear the Gospel proclaimed at Mass, we trace a small sign of the cross on our foreheads, on our lips, and over our hearts. This gesture is an act of faith by which we implore the Lord to let the Good News fill and transform our thinking, our speech, and our wills. These three human faculties correspond to the three classic Christian expressions of prayer: meditation, vocal prayer, and contemplation. All of them are rooted in the richness of God's Word.

Divine and Human Communication

In order to understand the most fundamental of these three forms — vocal prayer — we must turn our attention to the deepest meaning of the Incarnation. St. John tells us: "In the beginning was the Word. . . . Whatever came to be in him found life. . . . The Word became flesh and made his dwelling among us, and we have seen his glory" (cf. Jn 1:1-14). John the Evangelist describes the Incarnation as a type of sacred utterance in which God speaks so as to become one of us.

In this wondrous mystery we discover two crucial properties of discourse. First of all, it is through speech that we share the essence of ourselves with others. The Word of God proceeds from the Godhead and becomes manifested as a Divine Person who longs to make himself known to us. We are called to repeat this dynamic, which God reveals. Through the spoken word that proceeds from the hidden depths of ourselves, we manifest our personhood to others. Speech is a free revelation of our inner personality to others. By our conversation, we share with others our interior life in a manner redolent of the Trinity. Only words offered in loving communication can adequately express the true beauty, dignity, and meaning of our life as human persons. As Von Balthasar puts it, "when God becomes man then man as such becomes the expression, the valid and authentic expression of the divine mystery."

At the same time, it is by speaking with others that we bind ourselves to them and grow in greater unity. The spoken word forms people into intimate, close-knit communion, for speech is an integrating part of our very being. In reflecting on the alienation of her own blindness and deafness, Helen Keller wrote: "When we walk in the valley of twofold solitude we know little of the tender affections that grow out of endearing words and actions and companionship." The words we utter are not static and lifeless, but creative and generative. Von Balthasar wrote: "Speech intends life. It intends action and making. It is already incipient deed and goes beyond itself in works and in involvement with life."

The coming of Jesus, then, is a kind of divine communication — the beginning of a conversation that we are called to continue. "Whoever belongs to God hears the words of God. . . . Whoever loves me will keep my word" (Jn 8:47; 14:23). One important way that we remain true to God's Word is by responding to what we hear from him in the form of vocal prayer. By expressing ourselves in vocal prayer we recognize more deeply how our personhood images the three Persons of the blessed Trinity. It is the way that we open up and hand over the depths of ourselves to God. On the cross, Jesus "cried out again in a loud voice, and gave up his spirit" (Mt 27:50). Our heartfelt vocal prayer participates in that ultimate and saving self-offering.

The Many Uses of Prayer

In vocal prayer we discover how our lives of faith express the very holiness of God. Vocal prayer deepens our union with the Lord and intensifies our communion with his Church. It galvanizes our faith-convictions and compels us to turn our words into generous and compassionate action. In the process, we realize how very true it is that " 'one does not live by bread alone, / but by every word that comes forth from the mouth of God' " (Mt 4:4).

In prompting us to vocal prayer, God satisfies an innate longing in us. The Catechism teaches that "The need to involve the senses in interior prayer corresponds to a requirement of our human nature. We are body and spirit, and we experience the need to translate our feelings externally. We must pray with our whole being to give all power possible to our supplication" (2702). In other words, it is not that God "needs" our vocal prayer, but rather that praying vocally significantly helps us.

Helen Keller recalls the mystical moment in which Anne Sullivan succeeded in teaching her how to verbalize: "That living word awakened my soul, gave it light, hope, joy, set it free! There were barriers still, it is true, but barriers that could in time be swept away. I saw everything with the strange, new sight that had come to me."

Our ability to name God and to give expression to the profound mysteries of salvation is meant to produce in us that same euphoria of light, hope, joy, and liberation. Every privileged instance of vocal prayer centered in God's Word is a new moment of awakening, release, and new vision.

Practically speaking, vocal prayer assists us in several ways. It builds us up and strengthens us when our faith begins to flag. This is one of the reasons why Jesus himself prays vocally: "Father . . . I know that you always hear me; but because of the crowd here I have said this" (Jn 11:41, 42). When we witness the vocal prayer of others, especially at Mass, the administration of the sacraments, and the Liturgy of the Hours, our life of faith never fails to become bolstered and renewed. In turn, the witness we give to others by our practice of vocal prayer immeasurably uplifts our brothers and sisters in need in the way that the prayers of the saints constantly support us.

The vocal aspect of our prayer helps to make our piety more complete. God "wants the external expression that associates the body with interior prayer, for it renders him that perfect homage which is his due" (2703). It is not enough to hold our prayer within. For every prayer is offered to God as a sacrifice of our deepest selves. And when we do not know what to say in offering that sacrifice, God helps us, "for we do not know how to pray as we ought, but the Spirit itself intercedes with inexpressible groanings" (Rom 8:26).

Vocal prayer is also instrumental in bringing together the people of God. "Because it is external and so thoroughly human, vocal prayer is the form of prayer most readily accessible to groups" (2704). The communitarian aspect of vocal prayer encourages others to take part in the worship of God in a nonthreatening yet immensely effective and enriching manner. The wisdom of the Church in this regard is manifested in the abundant treasury of prayer that has been preserved and handed down through the centuries, especially the rosary, novenas, blessings, litanies, and myriad devotional prayers.

Of course, the Lord's words must remain close to our hearts whenever we engage in vocal prayer: "In praying do not babble like the pagans, who think that they will be heard because of their many words" (Mt 6:7). The Catechism instructs us that, in praying vocally, "it is most important that the heart should be present to him to whom we are speaking in prayer" (2700). For when our heart is fully engaged and focused on God, then "vocal prayer becomes an initial form of contemplative prayer" (2704).

Just as Jesus, the Word of God, became flesh, so by devout words, "our prayer takes flesh" (2700). We rely, then, on vocal prayer to enable us to find life by coming to be in the Word who is Jesus.

Chapter 23

Meditation

CATECHISM OF THE CATHOLIC CHURCH ¶2705 - ¶2708

The Catechism describes meditation as "above all a quest. The mind seeks to understand the why and how of the Christian life, in order to adhere and respond to what the Lord is asking" (2705). And what the Lord asks in a special way is that he be known by us: "By revealing himself God wishes to make [men] capable of responding to him, and of knowing him, and of loving him far beyond their own natural capacity" (52). In meditation, we take advantage of the riches of revelation — especially Sacred Scripture — in order to respond to God's offer of love and intimacy in a way that exceeds our own feeble means.

The Essence of Christian Meditation

Meditation is a gift and a privilege. As we embark on the quest of meditation, we follow in the way of the Blessed Mother who, as she witnessed the worship of shepherds before her infant Son, "kept all these things, reflecting on them in her heart" (Lk 2:19). Similarly, upon finding the boy Jesus in the temple after three days of sorrowful searching, "his mother kept all these things in her heart" (Lk 2:51). Meditation is the way we recall and renew the graces that perfect our relationship with God.

The essence of all Christian meditation is reverent remembering. At the Last Supper, in offering the disciples his Body and his Blood, Jesus commands them: "Do this in memory of me." The Lord knows well our inclination to forget, to become absentminded, to lose focus. Christ gives the Church the Eucharist as a memorial to keep us mindful of the way to salvation by directing our thoughts to the passion and resurrection. In this sacrifice we grasp the dynamic at work in all meditation.

The Lord shows great solicitude in providing this way of purifying our minds and keeping our thoughts on the things of God. For, as he acknowledges, "from the fullness of the heart the mouth speaks" (Mt 12:34). Therefore, we are obliged to "have the mind of Christ" (I Cor 2:16) in order to know how to speak and act in the world. Meditation elevates our spirits and fills our minds with the truth and holiness of Jesus, enabling us to fulfill the instructions of St. Paul: "Set your heart on what pertains to higher realms. . . . Be intent on things above rather than on things of earth" (cf. Col 3:1-2).

This same concern inspires the very method Jesus uses to teach us about God's kingdom. The parables compel us to profound meditation. By their design, the parables force us to think, to analyze, to make judgments, to apply our freedom, to engage our passions, to question, to ponder, to argue, to assent.

Every Christian who makes meditation a personal priority is like the good steward of the Gospel. After relating the parables of the kingdom, Jesus asks: "Do you understand all these things?" This is the question underlying each moment that we meditate on the Christian mystery. For "every scribe who has been instructed in the kingdom of heaven is like the head of a household who brings from his storeroom both the new and the old" (Mt 13:51-52). That is the point of meditation: to keep the truth of the Gospel firmly fixed before our eyes. Because of meditation, the Word of God and the events of salvation retain their relevance and urgency in our lives of faith.

The Effects of Meditation

At the same time, meditation brings about three important spiritual effects. Meditation enables us to appropriate the things of God. As the Catechism explains, "To meditate on what we read helps us to make it our own by confronting it with ourselves. . . . We pass from thoughts to reality . . . we discover in meditation the movements that stir the heart and we are able to discern them" (2706).

One ancient and esteemed method for such appropriation is *lectio divina* — the reverent, devotional reading of Scripture and other spiritual texts. This specialized form of meditation equates us with the seed the farmer sowed on good soil: "The seed sown on rich soil is the one who hears the word and understands it, who indeed bears fruit and yields a hundred- or sixty- or thirtyfold" (Mt 13:23). Like the seed that grows into a robust plant, through meditation the Word of God takes root in us, blossoms, and becomes fruitful.

Through meditation we also identify more deeply with Jesus. "Christians owe it to themselves to develop the desire to meditate regularly. . . . The important thing is to advance, with the Holy Spirit, along the one way of prayer: Christ Jesus" (2707).

One of the great masters of Christian meditation, St. Ignatius of Loyola, suggests this method of praying: "The person praying should say the word 'Father,' and continue to consider the word as long as meanings, comparisons, relish, and consolations connected with it are found. The same procedure should be continued with each word of the Our Father, or of any other prayer which one wishes to use in this manner. . . . If one finds in one or two words matter which yields thought, relish, and consolation, one should not be anxious to move forward, even if the whole hour is consumed on what is being found." Such concentration and commitment opens up to us powerfully the wonders of God's love, and enables us to unite ourselves more deeply to it.

And finally, by immersing what is most human about us in meditation, our personal conformity to Christ becomes intensified. "Meditation engages thought, imagination, emotions, and desire. This mobilization of faculties is necessary in order to deepen our convictions of faith, prompt the conversion of our heart, and strengthen our will to follow Christ" (2708).

Without the kind of meditation that produces recollection and rectitude, our own unredeemed thoughts take over and run wild. They conform us — not to Christ — but to the venal and selfish things of the world. Fervent meditation is one important way that we fulfill the command of Jesus: "You shall love the Lord, your God, with all your heart, with all your being, with all your strength, and with all your mind" (Lk 10:27). For then we find the way to "put on the Lord Jesus Christ, and make no provision for the desires of the flesh" (Rom 13:14).

Chapter 24

Contemplative Prayer

CATECHISM OF THE CATHOLIC CHURCH ¶2709 - ¶2719

It's easy for us to side with a malcontent Martha over the seeming idleness of her sister Mary. And yet Jesus insists: "One thing only is required. Mary has chosen the better portion and she shall not be deprived of it" (cf. Lk 10:38-41). That one required thing, that better portion is contemplative prayer.

The Gaze of Faith

The Catechism describes contemplation as "a gaze of faith, fixed on Jesus" (2715). Seated at the Lord's feet and utterly absorbed in the Lord's words, Mary is presented to us as the model of Christian contemplation. She fulfills what God commands through the voice of the Psalmist: "Be still, and know that I am God" (Ps 46:11; RSV).

This transfixed stillness focused wholly on Jesus bears all the earmarks of one deeply in love. People in love long to be with one another. In contemplation we experience and satisfy this same desire as it is directed toward God. Contemplative prayer is the deepest union of our heart with the Heart of Jesus. The author of the *Cloud of Unknowing* calls it the "work of love," for in contemplative prayer we give ourselves completely and ardently to God.

As for those in love, in contemplation it is enough just to be with God and to be ourselves with God. "We let our masks fall and turn our hearts back to the Lord who loves us, so as to hand ourselves over to him" (2711). And in the process we come to appreciate how much we belong to him: "My lover belongs to me and I to him" (Sgs 6:3).

Contemplative prayer liberates us from the frantic and frenetic distractions of life. The modern world is quick to misjudge contemplation as a futile and foolish waste of time. But, as St. John of the Cross wisely instructs us: "The spiritual person should learn to remain in God's presence with a loving attention and a tranquil intellect, even though he seems to himself to be idle. For little by little and very soon the divine calm and peace with a wondrous, sublime knowledge of God, enveloped in divine love, will be infused into his soul. He should not interfere with forms or discursive meditations and imaginings. Otherwise his soul will be disquieted and drawn out of its peaceful contentment to distaste and repugnance. And if, as we said, scruples about his inactivity arise, he should remember that pacification of soul (making it calm and peaceful, inactive and desireless) is no small accomplishment."

The one in love eagerly listens to the beloved's every word, delighting in his voice, eager to respond. At the Annunciation, the Blessed Mother demonstrates this profound aspect of contemplative union. Mary's personal response to the message of the angel is the surrender of her entire will, her *Fiat,* offered as a sacrifice of love, in gratitude for the grace of receiving God's Word.

The Prayer of Quiet

But the lover also enjoys great ease and delight in sharing silence with the loved one. St. Teresa of Ávila refers to contemplative prayer as the "prayer of quiet." Such silence serves to enhance our ability and eagerness to listen to our beloved. Catherine de Hueck Doherty once wrote: "True, silence is sometimes the absence of speech — but it is always the act of listening. The mere absence of noise (which is empty of our listening to the voice of God) is not silence. A day filled with noise and voices can be a day of silence, if the noises become for us the echo of the presence of God. When we speak of ourselves and are filled with ourselves, we leave silence behind. When we repeat intimate words of God that he has left within us, our silence remains intact."

Authentic silence accommodates attentiveness, as the Eastern theologian Theophan the Recluse observes: Contemplative prayer, taking deep root in the heart, may be without words or thought: it may consist only in a standing before God, in an opening of the heart to him in reverence and love. It is a state of being irresistibly drawn within to stand before God in prayer."

In this silence, the one in love remains perfectly content just to behold the beloved, gazing upon him in a state of holy and tranquil abiding. The more we direct our sight, our energy, and our attention to Jesus, the less preoccupied we become with ourselves and our own self-centered concerns. The essayist Pico Iyer contends: "We have to earn silence, then, to work for it: to make it not an absence but a presence; not emptiness but repletion. Silence is something more than just a pause; it is that enchanted place where space is cleared and time is stayed and the horizon itself expands. In silence, we often say, we can hear ourselves think; but what is truer to say is that in silence we can hear ourselves not think, and so sink below ourselves into a place far deeper than mere thought allows. In silence, we might better say, we can hear someone else think."

Contemplation and Love

As we lovingly hold our gaze on the Lord, Jesus returns the look of love to us in a way that transforms us: "Jesus looked at him with love" (cf. Mk 10:21). The Catechism tells us that our "focus on Jesus is a renunciation of self. His gaze purifies our heart; the light of the countenance of Jesus illumines the eyes of our heart and teaches us to see everything in the light of his truth and his compassion for all men" (2715).

The intimacy shared by those in love mutually strengthens their confidence in the bond of love. Holy contemplation accommodates this intimacy between ourselves and God. It transforms our self-perception, so that the love of God for us becomes the truest standard for our self-assessment. We see and know ourselves as deeply loved persons. And that conviction colors the way we regard everything else.

This dimension of contemplation particularly assists us in our recurring need for repentance. For, as the Catechism points out, "Contemplative prayer is the prayer of the child of God, of the forgiven sinner who agrees to welcome the love by which he is loved and who wants to respond to it by loving even more" (2712). We succeed in loving even more when we share the very love of God with others in acts of charity.

The motto of the Dominican Friars is "contemplate, and then share with others the fruits of contemplation." Delight in divine love is contemplation's first and richest fruit. Once it is possessed in contemplative prayer, it in turn informs and perfects our every action. As St. Thérèse of Lisieux notes: "It is no longer a question of loving one's neighbor as oneself but of loving him as he, Jesus, has loved him, and will love him to the consummation of the ages." For this reason, the Catechism also describes contemplation as "a communion of love bearing Life for the multitude" (2719).

The person in love remains vigilantly attentive to every movement, every gesture, every attitude of the beloved. In contemplative prayer we offer this same solicitude and self-donation to God. We yearn to return to contemplation as often as possible so as to imbibe more deeply of God's holy love. In that act we experience our own self-perfection. A saint of the East, Dimitri of Rostov, once wrote: "As a flame increases when it is constantly fed, so prayer, made often, with the mind dwelling ever more deeply in God, arouses divine love in the heart. And the heart, set on fire, will warm all the inner man, will enlighten and teach him, revealing to him all its unknown and hidden wisdom, and making him like a flaming seraph, always standing before God within his spirit, always looking at him within his mind, and drawing from this vision the sweetness of spiritual joy."

For the ultimate desire of one who has tasted the joy of authentic love is to deepen that union of love with the beloved. The more we do so, the more we are personally transformed. The spiritual director of St. Elizabeth of Hungary testified to her holiness when he wrote: "I declare before God that I have seldom seen a more contemplative woman. When she was coming from private prayer, some religious men and women often saw her face shining marvelously and light coming from her eyes like the rays of the sun."

We can expect the same from our own devotion to God in contemplation. The unknown author of *The Cloud of Unknowing* understood well the sanctifying effects of contemplation on one who truly and utterly loves God: "As a person matures in the work of love, he will discover that this love governs his demeanor befittingly both within and without. When grace draws a man to contemplation it seems to transfigure him even physically so that though he may be ill-favored by nature, he now appears changed and lovely to behold. His whole personality becomes so attractive that good people are honored and delighted to be in his company, strengthened by the sense of God he radiates."

Chapter 25

The Spirituality of the Hail Mary

CATECHISM OF THE CATHOLIC CHURCH ¶2673 - ¶2682

Pope Paul VI once wrote: "Knowledge of the true Catholic doctrine regarding the Blessed Virgin Mary will always be a key to the exact understanding of the mystery of Christ and of the Church. . . . The Church's devotion to the Blessed Virgin is intrinsic to Christian worship." In explaining this truth, Pope John Paul II writes: "Mary embraces each and every one in the Church, and embraces each and every one through the Church" (*Redemptoris Mater,* 47). For this reason, the Catechism asserts that the all-holy Virgin Mary is the "model and source" of the Church's example of holiness (2030).

Entering into the Mystery of the Annunciation

In our own striving for holiness, one invaluable way of deepening our knowledge of the doctrine of the Blessed Mother is through reflection on the prayer the Hail Mary. In this regard, St. Louis de Montfort once wrote in his *True Devotion to the Blessed Virgin:* "Since the salvation of mankind began through the Hail Mary, the salvation of each individual soul is linked up with this prayer. . . . It was this prayer which caused the Fruit of Life to spring up in this dry and barren world, and it is this same prayer, devoutly said, which must cause the word of God to germinate in our souls, and to bear the Fruit of Life, Jesus Christ. . . . This prayer is a heavenly dew which seeps gently into the soil of the human soul, to bring forth fruit in due season."

Therefore, to pray the Hail Mary is to reenact that mystical encounter between God and the Blessed Mother at the Annunciation, and to enter into it personally. By our prayer we unite ourselves to Mary at prayer, and thereby assume her worshipful spirit of humility, openness, and utter self-donation. Our likeness to the reverent and receptive posture of the Blessed Mother disposes us to participate in the very graces she received in the greeting of Gabriel.

The Catechism reminds us that "the Virgin Mary most perfectly embodies the obedience of faith" (148). By praying the Hail Mary we ourselves become conformed to the Blessed Mother's obedience. We in turn experience the fulfillment of God's Providence in our life by our sharing in Mary's prayer. "When we pray with and to [Mary], we are adhering with her to the plan of the Father, who sends his Son to save all men. The prayer of the Church is sustained by the prayer of Mary and united with it in hope" (2679; cf. LG, 68-69).

Gabriel's words of greeting bespeak God's own devotion to Mary: "Our prayer dares to take up this greeting to Mary with the regard God had for the lowliness of his humble servant and to exult in the joy he finds in her" (2676). Regarding this angelic salutation, St. Louis de Montfort writes: "It is the most perfect compliment you can offer to Mary, because it is the compliment which the Most High God Himself made to her, through an Archangel. . . . It is by this compliment, too, that you will infallibly gain her heart; if you recite the Hail Mary with proper devotion." Therefore, in much the same way that the priest at the Eucharist appropriates and gives voice to the transforming words of Jesus at the Last Supper — "This is my Body . . . This is my Blood" — so do we make our own the saving words of God whenever we pray "Hail Mary. . . ."

God Draws Close

The Annunciation, then, is God's invitation to Mary to participate in the divine plan of salvation. But this redemptive encounter is first of all an invitation to a life of prayer that enables Mary to respond to the promptings of God's grace: "The living and true God tirelessly calls each person to that mysterious encounter known as prayer. In prayer, the faithful God's initiative of love always comes first; our own first step is always a response" (2567).

God constantly extends this same loving, grace-filled initiative to us. As the very first paragraph of the Catechism makes clear, "at every time and in every place, God draws close to man. He calls man to seek him, to know him, to love him with all his strength." The Hail

Mary is given to us as a paradigm and reminder of God's unceasing offer of saving love and of our obedient, faith-filled response.

Every time we pray the Hail Mary we recall that "God never ceases to draw man to himself" (27). Mary remains the way that God draws close to his people so that we might seek him, know him, and love him through the Fruit of Mary's womb. As St. Louis de Montfort writes: "The inaccessible drew near to us, and united himself closely, perfectly, and even personally with our humanity, through Mary; and it is also through Mary that we can draw near to God and unite ourselves perfectly and closely to his divine majesty."

Full of Grace

Pope John Paul II notes that "the messenger greets Mary as 'full of grace'; he calls her thus as if it were her real name." The Catechism teaches us that "a name expresses a person's essence and identity and the meaning of this person's life" (203). To be "full of grace" is Mary's essence, her identity, and the meaning of her life. As "full of grace," "Mary is wholly given over to him who has come to dwell in her. . ." (2676). Mary's fullness of grace signifies her complete emptiness of self.

The Blessed Mother's desire to remain empty of everything outside of God testifies to the incomparable integrity of Mary's prayer: "The prayers of the Virgin Mary . . . are characterized by the generous offering of her whole being in faith" (2622). By our fervent praying of the Hail Mary, the "Fiat" of the Blessed Mother becomes our own; the prayer enables us to make a similar offering of self that purifies and perfects the whole of our spiritual life. In describing Mary's *Fiat,* the Catechism asserts: "This is Christian prayer: to be wholly God's, because he is wholly ours" (2617).

The confirmation that Mary is wholly God's and that she is wholly his is the angel's next revelation: "The Lord is with you." The Catechism enlightens us that "by revealing himself God wishes to make [men] capable of responding to him, and of knowing him, and of loving him far beyond their own natural capacity" (52). This is preeminently true in the life of the Blessed Virgin Mary. Through her Immaculate Conception, Mary is prepared to know, love, and possess God in a way that gloriously surpasses natural human capacity. She is blessed in this way so that, at the proper moment, Mary might reveal her Son to the world: "When the fullness of time had come, God sent his Son, born of a woman" (Gal 4:4).

Because of Mary's unique union with the Trinity, the unseen God miraculously becomes visible: "In Mary, the Holy Spirit manifests the Son of the Father, now become the Son of the Virgin. . . . Filled with the Holy Spirit she makes the Word visible in the humility of his flesh" (724). In Mary's revelation of the Son of God we become capable of knowing God, of responding to him and loving him in a way that exceeds our own natural capacity. "When God reveals Himself and calls him, man cannot fully respond to the divine love by his own powers. He must hope that God will give him the capacity to love Him in return and to act in conformity with the commandments of charity" (2090). The Blessed Mother is God's gift who gives us the capacity to respond to God's love in the way he deserves.

Therefore, the Lord is with the Blessed Mother since, as Pope John Paul II stresses, "in an entirely special and exceptional way Mary is united to Christ, and similarly she is eternally loved in this 'beloved Son.' " The Catechism helps us to understand how Mary's total devotion to the Eternal Word becomes the very cause of her blessedness: "Mary is 'blessed among women' because she believed in the fulfillment of the Lord's word" (2676).

In the Name of Jesus

The first fruit of the fulfillment of God's Word in Mary is the gift to her of the holy name of Jesus. "The name 'Jesus' signifies that the very name of God is present in the person of his Son. It is the divine name that alone brings salvation, and henceforth all can invoke his name, for Jesus united himself to all men through his Incarnation, so that 'there is no other name under heaven given among men by which we must be saved' " (432; Acts 4:12; cf. 9:14; Jas 2:7).

The revelation of the name of Jesus to Mary — and to us whenever we prayerfully repeat the angel's words — signals a privileged grace of election. As the Catechism explains: "To disclose one's name is to make oneself known to others; in a way it is to hand oneself over by becoming accessible, capable of being known more intimately and addressed personally" (203). Elsewhere we read: "Our prayer . . . has access to the Father only if we pray 'in the name' of Jesus. The sacred humanity of Jesus is therefore the way by which the Holy Spirit teaches us to pray to God our Father" (2664), for "the one name that contains everything is the one that the Son of God received in his Incarnation: Jesus. To pray 'Jesus' is to invoke him and to call him within us. His name is the only one that contains the presence it signifies" (2666). Through Mary, then, we receive the Holy Name of Jesus by which the Lord manifests himself to us, hands himself over to us, and beckons us to know him personally and intimately.

Pray for Us

In the prayer, we next implore the Blessed Mother to pray for us. That petition is an act of hope, for we recognize that "By entrusting ourselves to her prayer, we abandon ourselves to the will of God together with her" (2677). It also stands as an act of faith in the power of Mary as intercessor. Pope John Paul II has written: "Mary places herself between her Son and mankind in the reality of their wants, needs, and sufferings. She puts herself 'in the middle,' that is to say she acts as a mediatrix not as an outsider, but in her position as mother. She knows that as such she can point out to her Son the needs of mankind and in fact, she 'has the right' to do so. . . . As a mother she also wishes the messianic power of her Son to be manifested, that salvific power of his which is meant to help man in his misfortunes, to free him from the evil which in various forms and degrees weighs heavily upon his life."

Central to this insight is the reality of Mary's maternal mediation, for we venerate her as "Mother of God." In this respect, our every utterance of the Hail Mary becomes an act of love. As Pope John Paul II insists, "Mary is not only the model and figure of the Church; she is much more. For, 'with maternal love she cooperates in the birth and development' of the sons and daughters of Mother Church. The Church draws abundantly from this cooperation . . . from the maternal mediation which is characteristic of Mary."

In asking Mary to pray for us, we are charged to accept the gift Christ made to the apostle John from the cross: we are to receive Mary as our Mother into our homes, into our lives. The Holy Father writes: "Mary's motherhood is a gift which Christ himself makes personally to every individual. . . . Entrusting himself to Mary in a filial manner, the Christian . . . brings the Mother of Christ into everything that makes up his inner life."

Our devotion to Mary as the Mother of God and our Mother remains indispensable for our life of faith, for the "motherhood of Mary in the order of grace continues uninterruptedly" (969; LG, 62). The Catechism teaches us: "Ever since the Cross, Mary's motherhood has extended to the brothers and sisters of her Son" (2674); "the Holy Mother of God continues in heaven to exercise her maternal role on behalf of the members of Christ" (975). Guerric of Igny explains that, although Mary's "womb carried a child once only, it remains ever fruitful, never ceasing to bring forth the fruits of her motherly compassion." We are the fruits of her womb.

By receiving Mary as our Mother, we dispose ourselves to the grace of spiritual childhood so essential to our eternal happiness: "To become a child in relation to God is the condition for entering the kingdom. For this, we must humble ourselves and become little. Even more: to become 'children of God' we must be 'born from above' or 'born of God' " (526; Jn 3:7; 1:13-11:12; cf. Mt 23:12). By praying to Mary, and by entering into the prayer of Mary, we realize how "prayer is the living relationship of the children of God" with the Trinity (2565). And just as the Son of God "learns to pray from his mother" (2599), so too do we gain an inestimable lesson in the Hail Mary.

To conclude with the insight of St. Louis de Montfort: "I have no more effective way of discovering whether a person is of God, than by inquiring whether he loves to say the Hail Mary. . . . The Hail Mary has been the means whereby the whole world was saved."

Chapter 26

Problems in Prayer

CATECHISM OF THE CATHOLIC CHURCH ¶2725 - ¶2745

The Catechism refers to prayer as a "battle" conjoined to "the spiritual battle of the Christian's new life" (2725). As such, prayer is comprised of numerous difficulties and obstacles that must be surmounted in order to insure progress in the life of faith. These problems confront the Christian before, during, and after the act of prayer.

Mistaken Ideas About Prayer

We encounter the most fundamental problems with prayer before we ever enter into it. The most basic of these is our mistaken notion of what prayer is. In essence, prayer is "a vital and personal relationship with the living and true God" (2558). Trouble comes when we attempt to conceptualize prayer apart from its relational character. When we reduce prayer to mechanical, psychological, cerebral, or merely ritualistic categories, we degrade the integrity of prayer. We thereby turn it into something sterile by objectifying God and his role in our prayer. To know what true prayer is, we must give ourselves to an authentic relationship with God.

Closely allied to this basic difficulty is the problem of entertaining false expectations about what prayer does. They tempt us to equate fervor with feelings. We might expect to experience physically some sensate response to our prayer. We might expect — unreasonably — immediate, almost magical results from our prayer. We might expect prayer spontaneously to change our life and the lives of others in a way that dispenses us from exercising the personal responsibility required to mature in charity and holiness. However, although at times God does bless us with a kind of tangible consolation in prayer, our ultimate expectations in prayer must exceed anything we can feel, any superstitious motives, and any notion that diminishes prayer to a simplistic panacea. The Catechism confirms the rectified expectation we should place on prayer: "Prayer restores man to God's likeness and enables him to share in the power of God's love that saves the multitude" (2572; cf. Rom 8:16-21).

Such mistaken conceptions may well be the by-products of collusion with the mentality of "this present world" (2727). The Catechism warns against the deceptiveness of rationalism, materialism, hedonism, and escapism so prevalent in contemporary society. These attitudes injure and contaminate faith and thereby cripple spiritual vigor. The Christian is called to see through the falsity of their claims and to reject them by putting on the mind of Christ: "Do not conform yourself to this age but be transformed by the renewal of your mind, that you may discern what is the will of God, what is good and pleasing and perfect" (Rom 12:2). Then, personally enriching prayer becomes possible as grace-filled renewal opens us up to saving knowledge, Christian values, ultimate delight, and unfailing hope.

Prayer and Repentance

However, we ourselves may need to accept responsibility for the difficulties we experience, especially if we attempt to approach prayer with unrepented sin on our soul. For prayer is as much a battle against ourselves as it is against the tempter. The *Catechism* reminds us that "We pray as we live" (2725). If our lives are marred by unconverted hearts and unconfessed sin, our prayer life will be the first to suffer. "Humility is the foundation of prayer" (2559), and true humility requires us to possess a right self-knowledge coupled with confidence in God's divine mercy that produces a healthy sense of sin. The integrity of our lives will be reflected in the satisfying integrity of our prayer. In turn, prayer will keep us on the way of righteousness, for "Prayer is an indispensable condition for being able to obey God's commandments" (2098). The rightness of our life in God "will depend on the rightness of our prayer" (2764).

Teach Us How to Pray

We may also encounter problems before praying simply because we do not know how to pray. This is no cause for shame. Jesus' own disciples needed to implore the Lord: "Teach us to pray" (Lk 11:1). Prayer is something that can be readily learned. If prayer seems daunting due to lack of knowledge of techniques, we need begin simply by following the lesson Jesus gave in response to his disciples' request — that is, to pray reflectively the Lord's Prayer which "is truly the summary of the whole Gospel" (2761). United with Jesus, and with that prayer in our hearts, we remain ever disposed to avail ourselves of other methods of enriching our prayer.

Distractions and Aridity

Several problems also arise during the act of prayer. The most basic and general of these difficulties is that of distraction. Distractions seek to lure us away from the Lord by enticing us to indulge our attention on things that attract us. Distractions can come at any moment, despite our fervent resolutions to concentrate on God. Perhaps the worst distraction is the impulse to decipher why we have any distractions in the first place. This only makes matters worse.

The Catechism supplies the best remedy: "To set about hunting down distractions would be to fall into their trap, when all that is necessary is to turn back to our heart; for a distraction reveals to us what we are attached to, and this humble awareness before the Lord should awaken our preferential love for him and lead us resolutely to offer him our heart to be purified" (2729).

A particularly volatile strain of distraction is temptation. The real danger of temptation lies in its ability to make us doubt ourselves, our convictions, and commitments. Trouble with temptation can lead us facilely and falsely to conclude that somehow we are displeasing to God. The truth is that God allows temptations in our lives only to strengthen our relationship with him. Temptations in fact serve us by revealing the areas of our lives in which we are weakest so that we can turn that weakness over to God, relying on his mercy. Ironically, temptations are a sign of divine election and of the promise of a special grace, as St. Paul instructs us: "God . . . will not let you be tried beyond your strength; but with the trial he will also provide a way out, so that you may be able to bear it" (I Cor 10:13).

The most trying temptation may be that of dryness, or aridity. Aridity is that unsettling state of experiencing no feeling, comfort, or sensate consolation in the process of prayer. Rather, it leaves us feeling abandoned, unheard, and alone. God seems very distant, removed, and aloof. Aridity can mean one of two things: either we have not given ourselves over to God as completely in faith as he requires. Or we have — and God's reward for such self-abandonment is the invitation to live deeply united to him in the darkness of faith without any reliance on created supports in prayer, like feelings. Therefore, contrary to what it may seem, aridity can signal a vibrant and fruitful life in Christ.

It is important to come to this understanding of spiritual dryness. For ignorance of it can lead to something worse: *acedia*, "a form of depression due to lax ascetical practice, decreasing vigilance, carelessness of heart" (2733). The more common term for this is "sloth." However, the word is not meant to denote laziness so much as a reluctance to take delight in the things of God. When we fail to find our joy in the Lord, then in fact we do become lazy about the things of God as we stand "repelled by divine goodness" (2094). This pitfall returns us to the truth that the one essential trait in all authentic prayer is a rectified "composure of heart" (2699): "If our heart is far from God, the words of prayer are in vain" (2562).

When we embrace Jesus as "the only joy of every human heart," acedia recedes as our prayer intensifies.

Of course, we must not overlook the fact that it is possible for one to pray badly. The Letter of James warns: "You ask but do not receive, because you ask wrongly, to spend it on your passions" (Jas 4:3). True and pure prayer requires a wholeness of heart set on the things of God; "If we enter into the desire of his Spirit, we shall be heard" (2737).

One key element of authentic Christian prayer is faith-filled reliance on the intercession of the saints: "The Church . . . is the place where we know the Holy Spirit . . . in the witness of saints through whom he manifests his holiness and continues the work of salvation" (688). The saints perfect our prayer, for "those who dwell in heaven fix the whole Church more firmly in holiness. . . .They proffer the merits which they acquired on earth through the one mediator between God and men, Christ Jesus" (956). It is right and proper for us to rely on the saints in this way, for "When they entered into the joy of their Master, they were 'put in charge of many things.' Their intercession is their most exalted service to God's plan" (2683).

Sometimes we have problems during prayer because our prayer is not sufficiently Christ-centered. St. Paul admonishes: "But I am afraid that . . . your thoughts may be corrupted from a sincere [and pure] commitment" (II Cor 11:3). Authentic prayer "always presupposes effort" (2725), and the greatest effort involves relinquishing our self-centeredness, and centering ourselves on Jesus. Sometimes the greatest work and agony of prayer is just sitting still. Yet, "God wills that our desire should be exercised in prayer" (2737; St. Augustine, *Ep*. 130, 8, 17: PL 33, 500). Our devoted stillness before the Lord manifests our desire for him.

Problems After Prayer

We might also occasion problems after prayer. We may be led to conclude, that, since we do not see hoped-for results in praying, we have failed in prayer. The Catechism consoles us: "Do not be troubled if you do not immediately receive from God what you ask him; for he desires to do something even greater for you, while you cling to him in prayer" (2737; Evagrius Ponticus, *De oratione* 34: PG 79, 1173).

Some may go so far as to experience existential self-doubt due to seeming ineffectiveness in prayer. However, the right response is "to battle to gain humility, trust, and perseverance" (2728). To insure victory in our spiritual battles, the Letter to the Ephesians informs us how we should equip ourselves: "Put on the armor of God, that you may be able to resist on the evil day. . . . Stand fast, with your loins girded in truth, clothed with righteousness as a breastplate, and your feet shod in readiness for the gospel of peace. In all circumstances, hold faith as a shield. . . . Take the helmet of salvation and the sword of the Spirit which is the word of God" (Eph 6:13-17). Such personal armament dispels all doubt from us as our prayer takes on divine properties: "The weapons of our battle are not of flesh but are enormously powerful" (II Cor 10:4).

Chapter 27

The Spirituality of the Lord's Prayer

CATECHISM OF THE CATHOLIC CHURCH ¶2759 - ¶2865

The Catechism refers to the Lord's Prayer as the fundamental Christian prayer, the summary of the whole Gospel, the foundation of further desires, the most perfect of prayers, and the center of the Scriptures (2759, 2761, 2774). Yet, since we are so familiar with the Our Father, we wonder if we can gain any deeper insight into this most crucial prayer.

The Catechism sagely cites a passage of St. Thomas Aquinas on the Lord's Prayer: "In it we ask, not only for all the things we can rightly desire, but also in the sequence that they should be desired. This prayer not only teaches us to ask for things, but also in what order we should desire them" (2763).

If the Lord's Prayer specifies the principal values of the Christian life in order of their priority and importance, what might we learn by beginning at the end and working our way through the prayer in reverse order? Such an analysis manifests to us a kind of pattern and summary of spiritual maturity — the step-by-step progression by which many people typically grow in their relationship with God. This approach serves to help us better understand the structure and integrity of the prayer so as to deepen our relationship with God.

Deliverance From Evil and Temptation

Perhaps the most primordial of all human prayer is the final petition: "Deliver us from evil." This fundamental plea appears on the lips of even the most hardened unbelievers when threatened by danger, fear, or catastrophic need, making theists of us all. In a rudimentary way it serves as the start of the life of faith for, by our plea, we reject the impending evil, we acknowledge our inability to save ourselves, and we confess that God alone has the power to deliver us from it. That is, we open ourselves up to receiving God's mercy and grace.

As we mature, we readily see how the greatest threats in our daily life rarely menace us from without. Rather, we more often are forced to contend with a conflicting terror within, namely, temptation. And so we are led to pray: "Lead us not into temptation." This petition recognizes the common dilemma in life of being confronted with competing good (and bad) things, and it implores God not to allow us to take the way that leads to sin. It asks God to strengthen our human freedom so that we will make choices that fulfill his will for us, that enrich our personal dignity, and so contribute to our ultimate happiness.

The Divine Mercy

Our encounter with temptation only points up to us the truth of our own vulnerability and feeble vincibility before the world. In turn, it humbles us before God as we recognize his gracious offer of help to us in the midst of it. We know we do not deserve the gift of God's generosity; we are enlightened to accept the richness of God's compassion and mercy as the sole motive for our redemption. Imbued with this spirit, we are impelled to pray: "Forgive us our trespasses, as we forgive those who trespass against us."

At this point the prayer turns us away from anxiety about future temptation and evil, and it focuses us on the past. Specifically, the petition fills us with holy compunction over the actual evil we have ourselves committed. We begin to see how we need to be saved, not only from what might come, but from what has already transpired. From ourselves. This petition awakens in us a healthy sense of sin.

What makes it especially healthy is the way the prayer leads us to comprehend the communal dimensions of personal failing. Even our most private sins injure others at large and the community as a whole. Therefore, we should not expect to experience the reparative power of God's mercy in isolation. Rather, in order for divine compassion to be authentically appropriated by us, it must be first given away by us . . . precisely to those others who have given us offense. And this is the only demand that the entire Lord's Prayer makes of us.

In acceding to this commandment, we are blessed with the revelation of a tremendous truth: the Lord has called us to live in holy dependence upon one another. Just as our personal sin affects the good of all, so does our grace-filled offer of forgiveness effect the reconciliation of all God's people.

This is a crucial breakthrough moment in faith. For at this moment we unite ourselves to a solution for sin that does not come from ourselves or from the world. We reverence forgiveness as a divine gift of the resurrection. And in asking for that gift, we eagerly assume our part in dispensing divine mercy without limit.

Divine Sustenance

The wonder of forgiveness makes clear to us the reality of our own weakness apart from God. So we next pray for the strength and nourishment that only God can give and that we need to receive every day: "Give us this day our daily bread." Now we are no longer looking for extreme favors, but we are asking God for the mundane and ordinary. That is to say, our prayer has become a prayer of self-abandonment and self-surrender.

For the first time in prayer we deal with the here and now: today. It is a sign that we are living in the present moment. Attentiveness to the present moment compels us to remain open to receive all the love and caring the Father wants to pour into our lives. The reception of such divine beneficence depends upon our personal disposition. Unless we remain poor, humble, and hungry, God's bread will be wasted on us. Our petition, then, is voiced with the desire to reject every impulse of self-sufficiency and self-satisfaction.

Surrender to God

For what is this daily bread? "One does not live by bread alone, / but by every word that comes forth from the mouth of God" (Mt 4:4). This prayer for daily bread expresses our yearning for a fervent spiritual life. Therefore, we pray: "Thy kingdom come, thy will be done." In this brazen and daring act we renounce ultimate control over our lives, and we ask God's authority to govern us. We surrender all our willfulness and invite God to be the one who forms and refashions all our desires, and whose providence directs the plan for the way we live our lives.

The Catechism tells us that it is "the Father's will 'to raise up men to share in his own divine life' (LG, 2). He does this by gathering men around his Son Jesus Christ. This gathering is the Church, on earth the seed and beginning of that Kingdom" (541; LG, 5). By our petition we ask to be drawn into this sanctified gathering around Jesus and to share in God's own life. We turn over to God our mind and our heart. We profess God's sovereignty in a way that acknowledges our own vulnerability, but in a way that does not belittle us. Rather, calling for the fulfillment of the Kingdom and will of the Father stands as the hallmark and source of our true dignity.

God's Holiness and Majesty

Up until now we have praised God for all the things that he has done for us on earth. At this moment our prayer turns heavenly, praising God, not because of what he does for us, but because of Who He Is — the Majestic One. By praying that God is in heaven, we are claiming that he is present "in the hearts of the just" (2802). Our prayer signifies our desire to be one with the Father in his heavenly home. It is a prayer that we might be transformed and recreated so that our lives become 'heavenly' — that is, worthy dwellings for the Father.

We acclaim the Father's Name so that we might be made holy and blameless in his sight as we claim it as our own. We pray *Our* Father. In confessing God's holiness, we are asking to be made saints. This cry is a far cry from "deliver us from evil." The prayer acknowledges the efficacy of the Name of God in our sanctification. Jesus himself prays: "Righteous Father . . . I made known to them your name and I will make it known, that the love with which you loved me may be in them and I in them" (Jn 17:25-26). The Father loves Jesus as a Son . . . a child! If Jesus' prayer is to be fulfilled by having the Father's love live in us the way it lives in him, then the Father's love must live in us as his children.

Our Father

And so we pray: "Our Father." Now there is no plea, no petition — just a simple cry of love from a child. This was the way Jesus himself addressed God. His revealing and sharing this intimacy with us constitutes an earth-shaking privilege. In a certain respect, these two words are all that are needed, for they sum up the content and thrust of the rest of the prayer. To utter these two words we must be children and believe the way that God loves us as a Father: simply because we belong to him — because we are his.

As we pray "Our Father" we stand in amazement at the progress we have made in the life of faith. The servile fear that once enslaved us — "Deliver us from evil" — has now been transformed into filial fear. No longer are we threatened by impinging evil and terrifying punishment. Instead, the only thing we fear is the horror of ever losing God. Yet, even in this regard we remain steadfastly confident: "My Father . . . is greater than all, and no one can take them out of the Father's hand" (Jn 10:29).

Our maturity in faith inspires us to ever greater perfection: "So be perfect, just as your heavenly Father is perfect" (Mt 5:48). We achieve such perfection by fulfilling the end for which God created us: to be loving, receptive, generous, merciful, and thankful children of the Father. This method of assessing the Lord's Prayer persuades us that such perfection is possible for us, for "the Lord's Prayer *reveals us to ourselves* at the same time that it reveals the Father to us" (2783; cf. GS, 22).

Index

D

E

F

G

H

I

T

V